William G. Eliot

Discourses on the Doctrines of Christianity

William G. Eliot

Discourses on the Doctrines of Christianity

ISBN/EAN: 9783337260439

Printed in Europe, USA, Canada, Australia, Japan

Cover: Foto ©Lupo / pixelio.de

More available books at **www.hansebooks.com**

DISCOURSES

ON THE

DOCTRINES OF CHRISTIANITY.

BY

WILLIAM G. ELIOT

PASTOR OF THE CHURCH OF THE MESSIAH, ST. LOUIS.

TWENTY-SECOND THOUSAND.

BOSTON:
AMERICAN UNITARIAN ASSOCIATION.
1890.

CONTENTS.

INTRODUCTORY ADDRESS	5
UNITY OF GOD.	9
THE HOLY SPIRIT	27
OUR LORD JESUS CHRIST	39
OUR LORD JESUS CHRIST	58
ARGUMENT FROM HISTORY	83
THE ATONEMENT.	101
THE ATONEMENT	113
REGENERATION	127
RETRIBUTION	141

NOTE.

SHORT, simple, clear expositions of Christian doctrine, breathing a spirit of enlarged charity and devout reverence for the Sacred Scriptures, are always needed and always useful. The following Tract is the first of a series of discourses of this character recently prepared by the Rev. William G. Eliot of St. Louis, and preached to his own society in that city. The Executive Committee of the American Unitarian Association propose to republish the whole series in separate tracts, for distribution among their subscribers, and in such form that, when complete, the series will make a small, but interesting and useful, volume for general circulation.

INTRODUCTORY ADDRESS.

There are two popular errors concerning Unitarians, as a body of believers, which I am desirous of removing from the minds of all who read this book. First, it is supposed that we deny the existence of Mystery in religion, and that we refuse to receive any doctrine which we cannot perfectly understand. I should doubt if human presumption ever went so far, if I had not read somewhere the words of a philosophical believer, who said, "Where Mystery begins, Religion ends." In all departments of human inquiry we find mystery, that is, something hidden from us and beyond our present reach, and it would be strange if religion were an exception to the general rule. All the subjects of which it treats are, by their nature, beyond our perfect comprehension. We may learn something of them, we may obtain glimmerings of the infinite truth, enough for present guidance and comfort and encouragement, and that is all. God, Eternity, Immortality, Redemption, Accountability, Judgment, — what infinite verities do these words convey, yet how completely are we overwhelmed in their contemplation! There is not one of them that we can perfectly explain. Our own souls are an unfathomable mystery to us, and how can we expect to comprehend the nature of

God and of Christ, and all the secrets of the spiritual world of which we form a part? We have no such expectation and make no such promise. We come to the study of religious subjects with reverential feelings, hoping to learn enough for our salvation, not expecting to know all. But what is distinctly revealed we do expect to know, and as far as we receive distinct ideas we expect them to be consistent with each other. Mystery and contradiction are very different things. The former is something beyond our sight, or seen imperfectly. The latter is plainly seen to be untrue. It may concern subjects of which we know very little, but of *every* subject we know enough to see that two contradictory statements cannot both be true. We know very little, for example, about electricity; but if any one were to say that it is a self-moving and independent power, and also an agent which never moves except by our will, we should answer, that, although the subject is one enveloped in mystery, the statement concerning it is manifestly false. Applying this to religious things: The union between God and Christ is a subject beyond our perfect comprehension — it is therefore a mystery; but as Christ has declared that he could " do nothing of himself," — that he " spake not of himself," but only " as the Father gave him commandment," — we are prepared to see that those who assert that he was equal with the Father, and independent in his authority, are in error. The subject is mysterious, but the contradiction is plain. So when Christ asserts that he did not know of a certain future event (see Mark xiii. 32), the assertion that he was nevertheless Omniscient, is evidently a denial of what he said. The limits of his knowledge we cannot define, but he plainly asserts that some limits do exist, which is a distinct denial of Omniscience.

The second error concerning us is of a like kind. It is

often said that we set Reason in opposition to Revelation, or above it, and that therefore we do not come to Scripture with a teachable spirit. This is not true, nor is any thing like it true. We do indeed think that the Unitarian system of Christianity is more rational than what is commonly called Orthodoxy at the present day, and this is one argument for its truth; for, as Reason and Revelation are both of them God's work, there cannot be any real opposition between them. If we are sure of any doctrine that it is irrational or self-contradictory, we may be equally sure that it is not a revealed truth. Revelation may tell us a great many things which are beyond our discovery, and which we can but imperfectly understand; as when it tells us that God answers prayer, or that " he works within us both to will and to do of his good pleasure." It makes us feel that the Truth is *above us*, and that, however earnestly we may reach upwards, we cannot perfectly attain it. But at the same time it develops, enlarges, and strengthens our rational nature, while commanding us to believe. Christianity never tells us to stop thinking, but to " prove all things and hold fast what is good." We are not commanded to receive any doctrine without inquiry, but to " search the Scriptures daily to see " what is true, and of ourselves " to judge what is right." We ask no charter of freedom greater than this; but this charter we do claim, not only as rational beings, but as Christians.

The outcry against reason, made by many religionists, is not only unwise, but inconsistent with their own practice; nor are there any Christians who adhere more closely to the plain and direct meaning of the Bible than Unitarians. The doctrine of the Trinity is nowhere plainly taught in Scripture, nor can it be stated in Scripture words; it is a *doctrine of inference*, built up by arguments, and depend ing upon distinctions so nice and difficult that it requires a good deal of metaphysical acuteness to perceive them. A crusade against reason comes with ill grace from those who use it so freely. There is no such doctrine in the Unitarian system, but it would be puerile to deny that reason is used in our religious researches. We become Christians only by its use. There is no other means by which we can guard ourselves from gross superstition. We cannot use it too freely or too much, so long as we use it reverently and with prayer.

It only remains to say, that the following Sermons were delivered in the Church of the Messiah soon after its dedication. They were not prepared as controversial discourses, and do not pretend to be a complete discussion of the subjects introduced. In their preparation I must acknowledge my great indebtedness to two works, "Concessions of Trinitarians," and "Illustrations of Unitarianism," by that ingenious and learned man, JOHN WILSON, of Boston, formerly of England. To his industry I am indebted for a great part of my quotations from Trinitarian writers.

W. G E.

St. Louis, April 10, 1852.

UNITY OF GOD.

AND JEHOVAH SHALL BE KING OVER ALL THE EARTH: IN THAT DAY THERE SHALL BE ONE JEHOVAH, AND HIS NAME ONE. — Zech. xiv. 9.

THIS IS LIFE ETERNAL, THAT THEY MIGHT KNOW THEE, THE ONLY TRUE GOD, AND JESUS CHRIST WHOM THOU HAST SENT. John xvii. 3.

I HAVE selected the first of these two passages, because it not only contains the belief of the prophet in the Unity of God, but it is also a prophecy that, in the Messiah's time, the same doctrine should be more fully established: for he says, "In that day there shall be One Jehovah, and his name One," — words which convey the idea of absolute Unity as strongly as any words can.

The second passage contains the words of Christ himself, and declares with equal plainness the same doctrine. They are words spoken in prayer. "These words spake Jesus, and lifted up his eyes to heaven, and said, Father, the hour is come; glorify thy Son, that thy Son also may glorify thee; as thou hast given him power over all flesh, that he should give eternal life to as many as thou hast given him. And this is life eternal, that they may know thee, the only true God, and Jesus Christ whom thou hast sent."

When we consider that these are words of a prayer offered by Christ himself, — when we look at their great explicitness, at the distinction which they make between the Father and the Son, at the emphasis with which they declare the Father's supremacy, — we see how important they are in the controversy between the Unitarian and Trinitarian believer. For the act of prayer is in itself an admission of supremacy; and when, in that prayer, we find the distinct assertion that the Father is the ONLY TRUE GOD, by whom Jesus Christ was sent, there seems to be nothing else needed for the final and conclusive argument. If we try to imagine some method in which Christ could have put the controversy at rest, I think we could find none less open to objection than this. If such words, under such circumstances, can be explained away, it would be in vain to seek for others which will stand.

Having such authority to rest upon, we begin our inquiry this evening. My subject is the Unity of God, and I shall attempt to prove that it is the doctrine both of the Old Testament and the New. But as all Christians receive this doctrine in some form, it is necessary to state more explicitly the position we desire to establish. When we speak of the Unity of God, we take the word in its common meaning; we mean simple, absolute, undivided unity. We mean that God is one being, one person, one Infinite and almighty Jehovah, the Creator and Upholder of all things. We do not pretend to understand the nature of God perfectly. Both in his being and in his attributes he is far above our comprehension. But we find no sufficient authority in the Scripture for increasing the difficulty, by dividing the unity of his being into a trinity of persons; a distinction which is beyond our clear conception, and which seems to us to lead to hopeless contradiction: for by each person we must understand one who has existence, consciousness, will, and attributes of his own, and this is also the definition of a separate being. The more earnestly we seek to explain this apparent contradiction, that there are three and yet only one, three persons but one being, the greater the difficulty becomes; until we must end, as most persons do end, with saying that it is an unfathomable mystery, in which we must believe without questioning. Now we distinctly say, that, if the Scripture is so, we will try to believe it. We do not set up our reason against Scripture, which is the acknowledged revelation of God; but we must use our reason to search the Scripture before we can admit a doctrine so obscure and so difficult. We have a right to expect plain proof before we can be required to believe it. Upon this basis we proceed to consider the subject.

The Unitarian belief is, that there is one God, the Father Almighty, maker of heaven and earth. The Trinitarian believes that there is one God, Father, Son, and Spirit; that the Father is God, that the Son is God, and that the Holy Spirit is God, yet that there are not three Gods, but one God. Which of these is the true doctrine? You see the exact point of difference, and I cannot help here saying that we have this advantage: we can express our whole belief in unaltered Bible language. We believe in one God the Father; and the Apostle Paul speaks with us when he says, "To us there is but one God, the Father, of whom are all things, and we in him, and one Lord Jesus Christ, by whom are all things, and we by him." (1 Cor. viii. 6.) And again, when he says, "There is one God and Father of all, who is above all and through all and in you all." (Eph. iv. 6.) We say that the Father alone is the supreme God; and herein we have the testimony of Christ himself in the words of our text, " that we may know thee, the only true God, and Jesus Christ whom thou hast sent." It is very important, in the defence of what we believe, to say that no similar statement of the Trinitarian belief, concerning God, can be made in unaltered Scripture language. It seems to me almost fatal to that belief, because, being confessedly obscure and difficult, its plain statement is by so much the more desirable, and, if it were true, might be confidently expected from those who " declared the whole counsel of God." It is a very strong argument agains such a doctrine, that it cannot be expressed or explained without a departure from Scripture language. Let us turn however, more carefully to the law and the testimony.

We look first to the Old Testament, from which our argument is brief and conclusive. The great object of that dispensation, under Moses and the Prophets, was to establish the doctrine of God's Unity.

When Moses was appointed the leader of Israel, he found his people buried in gross superstition and idolatry. He led them forth from Egypt in the name of the great I AM the Jehovah, the God of Abraham, Isaac, and Jacob. He instructed them in the history of past times, and for this purpose the book of Genesis was written: to show that the God in whose name he spoke was the same God by whom the heavens and the earth were created, by whom the wickedness of men had in times past been punished, by whom a part of the human race had been saved from the general destruction, by whom their ancestors, Abraham and his children, had been greatly blessed, in that land of promise to which he was now about to lead them, and establish them there as a great people. When he brought them to the foot of Mount Sinai in the wilderness, after they had been rescued by the strong hand and outstretched arm of the Almighty, in the midst of the fire and the smoke this eternal truth was spoken: "Hear, O Israel, Jehovah thy God is one Jehovah." I use the word Jehovah, instead of Lord, because, as you know, wherever the latter is printed in capitals in the Old Testament the original Hebrew is Jehovah. Now this word is derived from HAYAH, to be, and means self-existence; so that the meaning is, "Hear, O Israel, the self-existent one, thy God, is the only self-existent."

That was the great central doctrine of the Jewish religion. They received it slowly and unwillingly; it was too grand for their degraded minds, and they returned again and again to the idolatries of the heathen. For a thousand years, their history is a succession of defeats and victories. So long as they held fast to their national belief in Jehovah as the only God, they were superior to all their enemies; but whenever they were corrupted by idolatrous practices they were shorn of their strength and brought low. Thus continued through the time of the Judges and of the Kings during which prophets were sent to them from time to time to reiterate the one great truth, on the preservation of which their existence as a nation depended. They declared it in the most emphatic language; they enforced it by threats of the most terrible punishment if it was forsaken, and by the most glorious promises if it was faithfully adhered to.

There would be no end to the task if I were to attempt to give quotations in proof of this. Let me offer, however a few as a sample: Deut. xxxii. 39, "See now that I, even I, am He, and there is no God with me! I kill and I make alive" Isaiah xliv. 8, "Thus saith Jehovah: Beside me there is no God: is there a God beside me? yea, there is no God; I know not any." Isaiah xlv. 5, and elsewhere, "I am Jehovah, and there is none else. To whom then will ye liken God, or what likeness will ye compare unto

2

him; to whom then will ye liken me, or shall I be equal? saith the Holy One; for I am God, and there is none else I am God, and there is none like me." If it were needful, we might bring several hundred instances as strong and conclusive as these; but those who are familiar with the Old Testament will not require it; they will admit that the great labor of all the prophets, from Moses till the time of captivity, was to teach the Unity of God and the purity of his worship. It is all a commentary upon the words spoken upon Mount Sinai, "Jehovah, thy God, is one Jehovah."

But their instructions were almost in vain. The people were still corrupted, again and again, by the nations around, until the judgments of God came upon them with more dreadful calamities. They were completely subdued and carried into captivity by the Assyrians and Chaldeans. There, in the land of strangers, when their harps were hung upon the willow, and they remembered with sadness the desolation of the temple of God, the eternal truth of God's Unity was indelibly impressed upon the heart of the Jewish people; it was burnt in by sorrow, never again to be erased. When a small remnant returned to Palestine, it was as the worshippers of one God, and to them the prophet Zechariah spoke, when prophesying of the Messiah's time, in the words of our text, "Jehovah shall be king over all the earth; in that day there shall be One Jehovah, and his name One." The nation had yet many calamities to endure, many vicissitudes of fortune; but among them all they never departed again from the lesson which had been so severely learned.

Such is a general view of the Old Testament, which is, I think, decisive of the question before us. If it had been intended by those who spoke under the inspiration of God, to convey some peculiar idea of unity, different from that which the word ordinarily conveys, as, for example, a Trinity in Unity instead of absolute unity, would it not have been somewhere distinctly expressed? Would the chosen people of God, whose special mission was to teach the truth concerning God's nature, have been left in ignorance of so important a doctrine as this? Would it not rather have modified all the instructions of the prophets, and appeared in all their teaching? But what hint do we find of such a thing? From Genesis to Malachi, where do we find a single expression which would convey to an unprejudiced mind such an idea?

To show how diligently the record has been searched for such passages, and with what small success, the words, " a threefold cord cannot be broken," and the passages in which the word holy is repeated three times, as, " holy, holy, holy Lord God Almighty," have been quoted and greatly relied upon by learned theologians, as a proof of the Trinity in Unity. When such trifles are relied upon, it is a tolerably good proof that sound argument is wanting. We scarcely need to be informed that the repetition of the word " holy " is only an evidence of intense feeling, as when David said in his affliction, " O my son Absalom, my son, my son Absalom!" or as in the exclamation of Jeremiah, " O earth, earth, earth, hear the word of Jehovah!" or as in Rev. viii. 13, " Woe, woe, woe to the inhabiters of the earth!" It is just as we would say thrice holy or thrice cursed; conveying intense feeling and nothing more.

We must also refer to two arguments, which, although they are abandoned by the most learned Orthodox critics, are still insisted upon by many persons. The first is, that the Hebrew word " Eloheem," translated God, is in the plural number, indicating, as is supposed, a plurality of persons in the Godhead. Our answer to this is the same which is given by John Calvin and Professor Stuart, whose orthodoxy will not be questioned, and is in these words: "For the sake of emphasis, the Hebrews commonly employed most of the words which signify Lord, God, &c., in the plural form, but with the sense of the singular." In proof of which, I refer to Exodus vii. 1, where the word *god* is applied to Moses, "And the Lord said unto Moses, See, I have made thee a god to Pharaoh." The Hebrew is here in the plural, and, literally translated, would be *gods*. A similar passage occurs 1 Sam. xxviii. 13, where the word *gods*, in the plural number, is applied to Samuel. In fact, this plural form to nouns of a singular number is a common idiom in the Hebrew language where intensity of meaning is expressed. The names of many of the heathen idols, as of Baal, of Dagon, of Ashtoreth, Beelzebub, and even of the golden calf made by Aaron, Ex. xxxii. 4, are all in the plural number. So in Gen. xxiv. 9, where it is said the servant put his hand on the thigh of Abraham his master, the word master is in the Hebrew plural, that is, *masters*. The same mode of expression occurs in other places, of Potiphar, of Pharaoh, and of Joseph, all of whom are spoken of in the plural number, as a token of unusual respect. I have before me no less than fifty instances, in which words having a singular meaning are in the plural form, according to the Hebrew usage. As in Prov. i. 20, "Wisdom crieth without; she uttereth her voice in the street"; the Hebrew word for *wisdom* is in the plural. In the same manner, I can give you instances in which the words salvation, love, truth, desolation, death, pride, and many others, are in the plural form in the Hebrew, though translated in the singular. These considerations are enough to show that the use of the word Eloheem is, according to Professor Stuart's explanation, nothing but a Hebrew idiom, upon which no doctrine of a plurality of persons can be built.

The other argument to which I refer is of a similar sort It is founded upon the words, Gen. 1. 26, " Let us make man in our image, after our likeness," which we also regard as an idiomatic mode of expression, commonly called the plural of excellence or of dignity. We can give instances in Sacred Scripture of its use by earthly kings, by Jesus Christ, by the Apostle Paul, and by many others. In 1 Thess. ii. 18 are these words : " Wherefore we would have come unto you, even I Paul, once and again, but Satan hindered us"; where the Apostle applies the pronouns, *we* and *us*, to himself. We might quote other passages showing the same use of the plural, but it is not needful, as the argument is abandoned by a large part of Trinitarian writers. Martin Luther, Grotius, Bishop Patrick, Dr. South, Dr. Samuel Johnson, Archbishop Whately, are all good Orthodox authorities, and all of them agree with us upon this point.

I do not know of any other arguments now used, to prove that a plurality of persons in the Godhead is hinted at in the Old Testament. One thing, very important, is certain, that, if any such hints were conveyed, the Jews never understood them. The presumption is, that they knew their own language, and it is certain they understood that the Unity of God was taught by their Scriptures in the most absolute and unqualified manner. Such was their interpretation of Moses and the Prophets at the time when Christ came. In all Palestine there probably could not have been found a single man or woman, who supposed that there was any distinction of persons, such as is now taught, in the Unity of God.

If, therefore, such a doctrine is contained in the New Testament, it must have been completely a new revelation to the Jews ; and not only new, but also strange. At first sight it must have appeared to them then, as it does now, subversive of their ancient doctrine. It would have been necessary, therefore, for the Saviour and his Apostles to state it very plainly, and to prove its consistency with the law of Moses. If we find no such statement, we may conclude that there was no such doctrine. Silence, under such circumstances, would be a full consent to the old Jewish belief in the Unity of God.

What shall we say, then, when we find that this doctrine is reaffirmed, over and over again, by Christ and his Apostles, in the strongest possible language, which is used without any explanation, or any hint that a peculiar sense is to be attached to the word One, when applied to God? No less than thirteen hundred and twenty-six times is the word *God* used in the books of the New Testament, without any explanation to guard us from what our Trinitarian friends would call a fatal error upon this which is the fundamental doctrine of religion.

This is a tolerably strong case; but a more careful examination will make it still stronger. Let us look at the teaching of Christ himself first, and then of his Apostles. Christ uniformly spoke of God as his Father, and of the Father as the only God. Almost his first recorded words are these: "Thou shalt worship the Lord thy God, and him only shalt thou serve." He prayed to God as his Father, and taught his disciples to pray in the same words: "Our Father, who art in heaven." Upon one occasion, when some one called him "good master," he answered, "Why callest thou me good? there is none good but one, that is God." Upon another occasion, when asked what was the first commandment of all, he commenced in the very words of the law spoken from Mt. Sinai: "Hear, O Israel: The Lord our God is one Lord; and thou shalt love the Lord thy God with all thy heart, and with all thy soul, and all thy mind, and all thy strength. This is the first and great commandment." Observe how solemn is this affirmation of the old doctrine; it is a reënactment of the great central law of the Jewish religion, without one word of amendment or qualification. Can we ask any thing more?

But we have more, if possible. If this were all, it might perhaps be argued that the word "God" includes the idea of tri-personality in the Father, Son, and Spirit; but the Saviour has forbidden such a construction by teaching us that the God of whom he spoke is the Father only. We once more refer to the words of our text, words of prayer to the Father: "This is life eternal, that they may know thee the only true God, and Jesus Christ whom thou hast sent." He speaks of himself, the Son, as a separate being, dependent on the Father. "Glorify thy Son, that thy Son also may glorify thee." Again, in his prediction of his heavenly exaltation he says, "Hereafter shall the Son of man sit on the right hand of the power of God." So when in the garden of Gethsemane he prayed to the Father, "Not my will, but thine be done." And on the cross, in the time of his last agony, "My God, my God, why hast thou forsaken me?" and yet once more, after his resurrection, he said to his disciples, "I ascend unto my Father and to your Father, to my God and to your God." Thus, through his whole ministry, he used the same uniform and familiar language. I ask you again to remember that this language was addressed to those who had no conception of any other doctrine than the absolute Unity of God. How must they have understood it? I think, just as we understand it now, when we say, "To us there is but one God, even the Father."

The Saviour's testimony is therefore the same with that of Moses. But although this is admitted by many Trinitarians, it is said that the revelation of the new doctrine was reserved until after the descent of the Holy Spirit at the day of Pentecost. Let us look then at the preaching of the Apostles at that time, and subsequently. We find it to be exactly the same; the same language is used concerning God, without any hint that it is to be taken in a peculiar sense. These are their words: "The God of Abraham, and of Isaac, and of Jacob, the God of our fathers, hath glorified his son Jesus, whom God hath raised from the dead." And again: "This Jesus hath God raised up. Therefore, being by the right hand of God exalted, and having received of the Father the promise of the Holy Spirit, he hath shed forth this, which ye now see and hear." This language is repeated in the first six or seven chapters of the Book of Acts, over and over again; and God is always spoken of without any qualifying word, as the only Supreme Being, by whom Christ was sent, raised up, and glorified. Does this look like the revelation of a new doctrine concerning God?

In the seventeenth chapter of Acts, Paul makes a distinct declaration concerning God. He found an altar in Athens, erected to the unknown God, and said, "Whom therefore ye ignorantly worship, him declare I unto you." Now, what is this declaration? "That God who made the world, and all things therein, is Lord of heaven and earth; that in him we live, and move, and have our being; that we are his offspring, and that he hath appointed a day in which he will judge the world in righteousness, by that man whom he hath ordained; whereof he hath given assurance, in that he hath raised him from the dead."

The time would fail me, to speak of all the instances of this kind. The Epistles are full of them. The common mode in which God is there spoken of is, as "the God and

Father of our Lord Jesus Christ"; as, for example, 2 Cor. i. 3, "Blessed be God, even the Father of our Lord Jesus Christ, the Father of mercies, and the God of all comfort." Again, Eph. iii. 14, "I bow my knees unto the Father of our Lord Jesus Christ." And, Phil. ii. 11, "That every knee should bow, and every tongue confess that Jesus Christ is Lord, to the glory of God the Father." Observe, that these passages not only imply the supremacy of one God, but they also declare that this one God is the Father only. The same God whom the Apostle elsewhere calls "the King eternal, immortal, invisible, the only wise God, who is the blessed and only Potentate, the King of kings, the Lord of lords, who only hath immortality, dwelling in the light which no man can approach unto, whom no man hath seen nor can see, to whom be honor and power everlasting." (1 Tim. vi. 15.) All these are words of the New Testament. I ask you again, Could they be made more explicit? If I, as a Unitarian minister, were to task myself in finding words to express the perfect unity and absolute supremacy of God the Father, could any words be found more conclusive than these?

It appears, therefore, that the language of the Bible is uniform, from first to last, on this subject. Moses and the Prophets, Jesus Christ, both before and after his resurrection, and the Apostles, both before and after the day of Pentecost, assert, in the same unqualified words, that the Father is the only living and true God.

Upon what ground, then, are we authorized to divide that absolute Unity? Suppose that we were to find two or three passages which seem to imply such a division. Ought we not to explain them, if possible, in accordance with the great prevailing doctrine? Ought we, for the sake of them, to introduce inextricable confusion into our ideas of God? I think not. When we have so strong a general case made out, we ought not to feel troubled by a few difficulties in detail. The language which we have quoted is so plain, that we cannot be mistaken in its meaning. We hold to that plain meaning, and by doing so we are Unitarians. I say this, not because the difficulties in our way are many or great, but because it is important for the young inquirer to take this position. He ought not to expect to explain every text of Scripture to his perfect satisfaction; some difficulties will still remain, but they ought not to trouble him, where the general conclusion is so well established. In the present case, however, the remaining difficulties are few.

There are but two texts of any importance which are supposed to imply the doctrine of a Trinity. The first is the form of baptism: " Go ye and baptize all nations in the name of the Father, of the Son, and of the Holy Ghost." But this teaches no Trinity of persons, much less of equal persons in the Godhead. On the contrary, the use of the word Son implies inferiority. The words mean that we should be baptized into faith in God as our Father, in the Son of God as our Saviour, and in the Holy Spirit as the guiding influence which proceeds from God. This comprises the whole Christian faith. It is sometimes said, that to be baptized in the Son is a proof of his deity; but it is not so; for Paul speaks of the Jews as having been baptized into Moses. Nor does it follow, because the three are spoken of together, that they are equal to each other; for in Numb. xxi. 5, 7, we read, " The people came to Moses and said, We have sinned; we have spoken against Jehovah and against thee." And again, 1 Chron. xxix. 20, " All the congregation blessed Jehovah, God of their fathers, and bowed down their heads, and worshipped Jehovah and the king." And 1 Sam. xxv. 32, "David said to Abigail, blessed be Jehovah, God of Israel, who sent thee this day to meet me; and blessed be thy advice, and blessed be thou, who hast kept me this day from shedding blood." You will observe the strength of this language. It is an ascription of praise, — first to Jehovah, God of Israel, then to her advice, and then to herself. But the ascription is to be understood differently in each case. So, when we read that they worshipped Jehovah and the king, we understand the first as supreme worship, and the second as the homage of respect. In all such cases, which are frequent in the Bible, common sense saves us from error. Although two or three subjects are spoken of in the same connection, it does not follow that they are spoken of in the same sense, much less that they are the same thing, or equal to each other.

Nor does it follow that the Holy Spirit is a person because we are baptized into its name. For, according to a common mode of expression among the Jews, the name of a thing often meant the thing itself; so the Rabbins speak of being baptized into the name of liberty, and the Samaritans circumcised their converts into the name of Mt. Gerizim.

If you feel any remaining doubt as to this passage, which is regarded as the great bulwark of the Trinitarian belief, I can refer you to a great many Orthodox authorities which admit the interpretation now given. Among them are the celebrated Erasmus, Dr. Wardlaw, Schleusner, Michaelis and Professor Stuart of Andover. They all of them declare, that, although the baptismal form will bear a Trinitarian meaning, it may also be interpreted differently without violence to the language

The other text to which I referred is 1 John v. 7

"There are three which bear record in heaven, the Father, the Word, and the Holy Ghost; and these three are one." Of which we say, first, if we admit its genuineness, it affords no argument against the doctrine of the unity. The Greek word translated *one* is in the neuter gender, and means, not one being, but one thing; which is, according to the use of Scripture, not identity, but agreement; as when it is said, "He that soweth and he that watereth are one"; or as the Saviour prays for his disciples, "that they all may be one, as thou, Father, art in me, and I in thee." It is so that the passage is interpreted by Calvin. He says: "The expression 'these three are one,' refers not to essence, but to consent; as if the Apostle had said, the Father and his eternal word and spirit harmoniously bear testimony to Christ. There is no doubt that the Father, Word, and Spirit are called one in the same sense as blood, water, and spirit, in the following verse." The same explanation is given by the celebrated Beza, one of the great Orthodox authorities; and McKnight, the author of an Orthodox commentary, has these words: "It was not to John's purpose to speak here of the unity of the heavenly witnesses, in respect either of their nature or of their number. I am therefore of opinion, that, when he wrote 'these three are one,' he meant only that they are one in respect of the agreement of their testimony, conformably to the use of the same phrase in other parts of the New Testament." With such authority, therefore, as that of Calvin, Beza, and McKnight on our side, to which I might add that of twenty-two others, equally distinguished as Trinitarians, whose names I have now before me, we need not hesitate to give a Unitarian explanation to this famous text.

Truth compels me, however, to add, that the text, such as it is, is spurious. It has no proper place in the Bible, of which we have the following proof: — "1. It is not contained in any Greek manuscript which was written earlier than the fifteenth century. 2. Nor in any Latin manuscript earlier than the ninth century. 3. It is not found in any of the ancient versions. 4. It is not cited by any of the Greek ecclesiastical writers, though, to prove the doctrine of the Trinity, they have cited the words both before and after it. 5. It is not cited by any of the early Latin Fathers, even when the subjects upon which they treat would naturally have led them to appeal to its authority. 6. It is first cited by Vigilius Tapsensis, a Latin writer of no credit, in the latter end of the fifth century, and by him it is supposed to have been forged. 7. It has been omitted, as spurious, in many editions of the New Testament, since the Reformation; in the first two of Erasmus; in those of Aldus, Colinæus, Zwinglius, and lately of Griesbach. 8. It was omitted by Luther, in his German version. In the old English Bibles of Henry the Eighth, Edward the Sixth, and Elizabeth, it was printed in small types, or included in brackets; but between the years 1566 and 1680 it began to be printed as it now stands, by whose authority is not known." With such evidence before him, Bishop Lowth says: "We have some wranglers in theology, sworn to follow their master, who are prepared to defend any thing, however absurd, should there be occasion. But I believe there is no one among us, in the least degree conversant with sacred criticism, and having the use of his understanding, who would be willing to contend for the genuineness of the verse, 1 John v. 7."

You will see upon how slender a basis the doctrine of a Trinity rests. There is not a single passage of the Bible in which it is distinctly stated, not one in which it is clearly implied. The doctrine of the Divine Unity, therefore, remains unimpeached. It is written all over the Old and New Testaments, just as it is written all over the works of God everywhere in the universe: " Hear, O Israel, Jehovah thy God is one Jehovah." This is life eternal, that we may know thee the ONLY TRUE GOD, and Jesus Christ, whom thou hast sent.

THE HOLY SPIRIT.

GOD IS A SPIRIT. — John iv. 24.

My subject this evening is the doctrine of the Holy Spirit. Last Sunday I attempted to show that the doctrine of the Divine Unity, unqualified and undivided, is taught by the Old Testament and New Testament Scriptures; that God is our Father, and that the Father is the only true God, — the God of Abraham, of Isaac, and of Jacob, and the God and Father of our Lord Jesus Christ. This is the foundation on which we rest our faith.

Those who impugn this doctrine, or who modify it by a Trinity of persons in the Godhead, attempt to prove that Christ, the Son of God, is *equal* with the Father, and, in some sense, the same with the Father; also, that the Spirit of God has a personality and attributes, separate from God the Father and God the Son. Having thus asserted these points separately, they join them together, under a modified doctrine of the Divine Unity, as a Trinity of persons in one God. The most important step in their argument is to prove the Deity of Christ, that is, his equality or identity with the Father, and it might naturally be expected that this would form the next subject of our inquiry. Such is the usual course; but I have two reasons for departing from it by taking the doctrine of the Holy Spirit first. In the first place, I think that sufficient prominence is not given to this doctrine in the Trinitarian controversy. It is too often taken for granted, or accepted with almost no proof. Trinitarians, if they can satisfy themselves of the Deity of Christ, consider that their whole work is done. Very few are aware upon what slender proof the separate personality of the Holy Spirit rests. Very few are aware of what is the fact, that this doctrine was not even asserted in the Christian Church, nor made a part of the creed, until the end of the fourth century, by the Council of Constantinople.

I wish this to appear; both that the importance of the doctrine, and the difficulty of receiving it in any other way than that in which we receive it, may be known. I wish it to appear that the Scripture language concerning the Holy Spirit confirms our view of the Unity; that no doctrine of the Holy Spirit can be found such as is necessary to establish the Trinity. If I can succeed in this, we shall then come to the consideration of Christ's nature, with a strong presumption that our view of him is correct; for I think that, if it plainly appears that a third person in the Trinity cannot be proved, very few persons will undertake to prove the second, and the doctrine of the Divine Unity will therefore become more impregnable.

I take this course also for another reason. There is no subject upon which Unitarians are more misrepresented than this of the Holy Spirit. Because we deny a separate personality, we are thought to deny the Holy Spirit itself, that is, to reject all belief in divine influences for the regeneration of the heart and guidance of the life. Many persons hold to the doctrine of the Trinity because they suppose that its denial would involve an error like this. They shrink from the Unitarian belief for the same reason. They feel the necessity of those heavenly influences which are the workings of the divine spirit, and from their faith in such influences their chief enjoyment in religion proceeds. Shall they give it up? Even if overthrown in argument, shall they yield all the blessedness of their religion? We say no. If such were the alternative, let the doctrine of the Trinity be adhered to, with or without proof. The necessity of the heavenly influence which the heart acknowledges would be proof enough.

But there is no such alternative. To deny the personality of the Holy Spirit, separate from that of the Father, is not to deny the Holy Spirit itself. So far as the doctrine is a practical one, or of any practical importance in the formation of the religious character, all Christians are agreed upon it. In God we live and move and have our being. He works within us both to will and to do of his good pleasure. He is more ready to give his Holy Spirit to those that ask him, than an earthly parent is to bestow good things upon his children. But all this is as true to the Unitarian as to the Trinitarian. Indeed, it seems to me more true; for we believe that the gift comes directly from a Father's love. There is no intermediate doctrine of a third person to confuse the thoughts. When we pray to the Heavenly Father, we feel that we are in living communion with him and he with us.

The Greek word translated Spirit in the New Testament is *Pneuma*, the literal meaning of which is wind or breath. The corresponding word in the Old Testament has the same meaning. Both words occur very frequently in this sense. When applied to God, or to any intelligent being they are commonly translated Spirit, sometimes by the word Ghost which, as you know, had exactly the same meaning at the time when the translation of the Bible was made. To give up the ghost is the parting of the spirit from the body, and the Holy Ghost is only another name for Holy Spirit. The Greek or Hebrew word is exactly the same in both cases. Now the question in controversy is, What does this term Holy Spirit mean according to Scripture usage? Is it a person in the Godhead separate from the Father, or is it intended to express as its general meaning the influences which proceed from the Father? This question must be decided by a careful examination of the Scripture.

There are three principal uses of the term Holy Spirit when applied to God in the Scripture which we must examine. 1. Sometimes it means God himself; 2. Sometimes the power, or some other attribute, of God; and 3. Sometimes (which is the most common use) the various influences which proceed from God.

First: It is sometimes used as another expression for God himself, just as the spirit of man is sometimes used for the man himself. Of this we have an instance in 1 Cor. ii. 11, "For what man knoweth the things of a man, save the spirit of man which is in him? even so the things of God knoweth no man, but the Spirit of God." As we should not think of saying that the spirit of man is here any thing but the man himself, so the Spirit of God is God himself. So it is said, Ps. cxxxix. 7, "Whither shall I go from thy Spirit, or whither shall I flee from thy presence? If I ascend up into heaven, thou art there"; where the phrase "thy Spirit" evidently means the same as thy presence, or thyself. Again, Isa. xl. 13, "Who hath directed the Spirit of the Lord, or being his counsellor hath taught him?" where the Spirit of the Lord evidently means the Lord himself. This is in accordance with the words of our text, "God is a Spirit."

The only intelligent idea that we can form of God the Father is of a spiritual being, or of an infinite mind, partly made manifest to us through his wonderful works. Just as our idea of a man is chiefly that of a spirit or soul, which for the present is joined to the body as the means of its development. In both cases the idea is indistinct and imperfect. We cannot perfectly apprehend the nature of spiritual existence, and in our efforts to do so we may easily become puzzled. But so far as we have any distinct conception of the being of God the Father, we think of him as an infinite, omnipresent Spirit. How much, then, is our difficulty increased, and how hopeless does the confusion of our minds become, when we try to think of a Spirit of God, having a personal existence separate from God the Father! For if the Father is himself a Spirit, it is to speak of the Spirit of a Spirit, and in fact conveys no idea to the mind. But if in such cases we take the Spirit of God as another expression for God himself, there is no difficulty.

The second use of the term "Spirit of God" is to express God's power, or some other attribute. When the Saviour said, Matt. xii. 28, "If I by the Spirit of God cast out devils," he meant by the power of God; as we find in the corresponding passage by another Evangelist, Luke xi. 20, "If I by the *finger* of God cast out devils"; in both cases meaning exactly the same. So in Luke i. 35, "The Holy Spirit shall come upon thee, and the power of the Highest shall overshadow thee," the exercise of the Divine power is intended.

Such modes of expression are quite common in the Bible. They are intended simply to express the exertion of God's power. Whatever God himself does, he is said to do by his spirit, or by his word, or by his hand, or by the breath of his mouth; all of which means substantially the same thing. See, for example, Job xxvi. 12, "He divideth the sea with his *power*, and by his *understanding* he smiteth through the proud. By his *Spirit* he hath garnished the heavens; his *hand* hath formed the crooked serpent." Or in Ps. xxxiii. 6, "By the *word* of Jehovah were the heavens made, and all the hosts of them by the *breath* or Spirit of his mouth; he spake and it was done, he commanded and it stood fast." All such language is perfectly intelligible if we receive it as different modes of expressing the exercise of God's power and wisdom; but if in such language we try to find evidence that the Spirit of God is a person separate from God the Father, it all becomes obscure. We might as well attribute personality to the Finger or the Hand of God. Here also, as before, the natural use of language leads us to the more intelligible doctrine.

There is one other principal use of the term Holy Spirit, to which I have referred. It is that which means the Holy Influence of the Deity on the minds of his servants, with the accompanying gifts and powers. This is by far the most common use of the term in the Bible, — perhaps in nine cases out of ten where it occurs. It is a use which confirms our view of the doctrine in dispute, and I think is inconsistent with any other. While I read a few of the passages, I would ask your close attention, that you may decide for yourselves upon this point, to which doctrine the language is most favorable. The Scripture says, that the Holy Spirit was "put within" Moses; that the spirit of the Lord was "put upon" the prophets, and other inspired persons; that the spirit of the Lord "fell upon" Ezekiel; that to the Apostles the Holy Spirit was "partially given," but that to Christ it was "given without measure"; that they "received" the Holy Spirit; they were "baptized" with the Holy Spirit and with fire; they were "supplied" with the spirit of Christ, and were made "partakers" of it. The Holy Spirit, or Spirit of God, was "poured out" or "shed forth" both on Jews and Gentiles. Believers were "sealed" with the Holy Spirit of promise. Jesus "breathed on them," and said, "Receive ye the Holy Spirit." In Luke xi. 13 it is said, "How much more shall the Heavenly Father give the Holy Spirit to those that ask him"; and in the parallel passage, Matt. vii. 11, the words are, "How much more shall your Heavenly Father give *good things* to them that ask him"; so that the Holy Spirit in this case is the same with the "good things," or the spiritual blessings, promised. We are taught to "walk in" the spirit, and that the "fruit of the spirit" is love, joy, peace, long suffering, and the like.

There are two instances in which the descent of the Holy Spirit was accompanied by a visible demonstration. Both of them are referred to as a proof of the personality of the Spirit of God, separate from the Father. They are undoubtedly the strongest instances to that effect which can be alleged. The first of them is at the baptism of Jesus, and the second at the day of Pentecost. In the former, it is said that "the Spirit of God descended like a dove, lighting upon Jesus, and a voice came from heaven saying, 'This is my beloved Son, in whom I am well pleased.'" It was an outward token of God's approbation; the visible appointment of Christ as the Messiah. It was to this that the Apostle referred when he said, speaking of this very incident, "That God anointed Jesus of Nazareth with the Holy Ghost and with power." Acts x. 38. Observe that expression, which is used as descriptive of Christ's baptism: "That God *anointed* him with the Holy Spirit." Is it not perfectly inapplicable to the idea of separate personality?

The other instance is at the day of Pentecost, of which

we find similar language used. The event is described by Peter as the pouring out of God's Spirit, and he declares that "Jesus, being by the right hand of God exalted, and having received of the Father the promise of the Holy Spirit, had *shed forth* that which was seen and heard." And he exhorts his hearers to "receive the gift of the Holy Spirit, the promise of which had been made to them." You will observe how strongly all this language confirms the view which we take of the doctrine, and how difficult to be reconciled with any other.

These, therefore, are the three meanings which belong to the "Holy Spirit," according to Scripture usage: 1. It is sometimes only another expression for God himself, as the spirit of man is another expression, in some instances, for the man himself. 2. Sometimes it expresses the power of God, or some other attribute; as when we read, "By his Spirit he hath garnished the heavens." 3. Sometimes, which is the most common use, it means the spiritual blessings, or influences, or good things, which the Heavenly Father bestows upon those who ask him. We have no hesitation in asserting most positively, that there is no passage in the Bible in which the words may not be explained under one of these meanings. There is no passage in the Bible where the Holy Spirit is spoken of as a Self-existent, Almighty, or Omnipresent Person, distinct from the God and Father of Jesus Christ. But, on the contrary, the language is generally such that it cannot be spoken of a person at all but must mean the influences which proceed from God the Father.

Upon what ground, then, are we required to renounce our belief in the Unity of God, or, at least, to modify it by the admission of a third person in the Godhead? The arguments are so few, that it will not take long to answer them

I have already given the meaning of the words used in baptism, Matt. xxviii. 19, as expressing our belief in God as our Father, in Christ as our Redeemer, and in the Holy Spirit as the sanctifying influence which comes from God.

The only other text to which I need refer is found Rom. viii. 26: "Likewise the Spirit also helpeth our infirmities, for we know not what we should pray for as we ought, but the Spirit itself maketh intercession for us, with groanings which cannot be uttered; and he that searcheth the hearts knoweth the mind of the Spirit, because it maketh intercession for the saints, according to the will of God." "It is surprising," says Mr. Peabody, "that this text should ever have been quoted as favoring the idea of the supreme independent divinity of a Spirit, which *intercedes*, that is, offers prayer, of course to some superior being." It is one of those texts which are difficult to explain, word for word, but of which the whole meaning is perfectly evident. The idea of the passage is, that "the devout soul, in all its infirmity and ignorance, will still be sustained, for it will still press to the mercy-seat; and that if it knows not what to ask for, and cannot shape its own supplications, God, knowing the earnestness and rectitude of its desires, will satisfy all its real wants."

The principal argument for the separate personality of the Spirit is found in the four passages which I have read to you this evening from John xiv., xv., and xvi., in which the divine influences promised by Christ to his disciples are personified under the name of the Comforter. I think that if it can be shown that this personification does not, according to common Scripture usage, imply literal personality, very little argument will be left.

What is the Scripture usage in this respect? A brief examination will show us that no mode of expression is more common than that in which inanimate objects and qualities are spoken of as if they were living beings, having personal properties and performing personal actions. Thus, " the sea and the mountains are represented as having eyes; the earth as having ears; a song, a stone, an altar, water, and blood, the rust of gold and silver, are spoken of as witnesses. The sword and arm of Jehovah are addressed as individuals, capable of being roused from sleep. The ear, the eye, and the foot, the law, righteousness, and the blood of sprinkling, are exhibited as speakers; and destruction and death, as saying that they had heard with their ears. In the language of Holy Writ, the sun rejoiceth and knoweth his going down; the deep lifts up his hands, and utters his voice; the mountains skip like rams, the little hills like lambs; wisdom and understanding cry aloud, and put forth their voice; the heart and the flesh of the prophet cry out for the living God. The Scripture is a seer and preacher; the word of Jesus is a judge; nature, the heavens, the earth, are teachers. God's testimonies are counsellors, his rod and staff are comforters; the light and the truth, and the commandments of God, are leaders or guides. Sin is described as a master, and death as a king and an enemy. Flesh and the mind are treated of as having a will; fear and anger, mercy, light, and truth, the word and commandments of God, are exhibited as messengers. Charity is represented as in possession of all the graces and virtues of the Christian character." *

Such is the usage of Scripture. It is so common that I may almost call it universal. Some of the instances to which I have now referred are also much stronger as personifications than that in which the Holy Spirit is personified

---

* Wilson's Illustrations.

as the Comforter. For instance, if you will read the thirteenth chapter of the First Epistle to the Corinthians, you will find that charity is spoken of as a living person, who "suffereth long and is kind, who envieth not, who seeketh not her own, is not easily provoked, thinketh no evil, rejoiceth not in iniquity, but rejoiceth in the truth, beareth all things, believeth all things, hopeth all things, endureth all things." I refer you also particularly to the ninth chapter of the book of Proverbs.

It is evident, therefore, that personification is a very common figure of speech in the Scripture, and we are perfectly justified in this mode of interpreting those passages in which the influences of the Holy Spirit are called a Comforter. We can fully account for the language, without the necessity of supposing literal personality; and we are confirmed in this view, because we find that the Apostles regarded the "shedding abroad" of the divine influences at the day of Pentecost as a fulfilment of the Saviour's promise. (Acts ii. 33.) These influences were to them "the Comforter," which brought all things to their remembrance, and qualified them to be the ministers of Christ.

It may perhaps still further confirm us in this view of he language, that, even if we should admit that the Comforter is a literal person, he is evidently not upon an equality with the Father or the Son; for he is *given by* the Father, he is *sent by* the Son, he is to speak only what he *shall hear*, he shall *receive* of Christ whatever he teaches; all of which expressions imply inferiority. And accordingly it is a fact in the history of the Church, that, for two hundred years after the personality of the Spirit was taught, his inferiority to the Father and to the Son was universally admitted.

We feel justified, therefore, in rejecting the doctrine of

the personality of the Holy Spirit as a third Person in the Godhead. The Scriptures do not teach it, but just the contrary. We reject it as a human device, by which great confusion is introduced into our ideas concerning God, and which is of no practical utility. Let me again say, however, that we do not reject the true and Scriptural idea of the Holy Spirit. We believe in the reality and necessity of a Divine Influence in the soul, and upon it we place our chief dependence. Our prayer is, that the Spirit of God may guide us aright, so that our present seeking after the truth as it is in Jesus may be blessed to our eternal salvation.

OUR LORD JESUS CHRIST.

HE SAITH UNTO THEM, BUT WHOM SAY YE THAT I AM? AND SI-
MON PETER ANSWERED AND SAID, THOU ART THE CHRIST, THE SON
OF THE LIVING GOD." — Matthew xvi. 16.

THESE words distinctly explain the subject before us this evening. The question asked is exactly that which we now ask, — Whom do the Scriptures say that Jesus Christ is? And the answer given is exactly the same which we, as Unitarian believers, would give. We take the words in their fullest meaning, and adopt them as the confession of our faith. "He is the Christ, the Son of the living God." In these words, not only the statement of our belief is contained, but also the argument on which it rests. The word "Christ" means anointed. It is in Greek, the same with "Messiah" in Hebrew, and implies that Jesus was anointed by God with the Holy Spirit and with power, to become a prince and a saviour, a prophet and a judge. It implies, therefore, very high distinction, but at the same time a distinction conferred by one higher than himself.

He is also "the Son of God"; a phrase elsewhere bestowed upon prophets and righteous men, but here used with peculiar solemnity, — "the Son of the living God," — and with peculiar meaning; the same as when he is called "the beloved Son," or "the only begotten Son of his Father." Such words, I think, announce peculiar exaltation, — peculiar nearness to God. I doubt if we can at present understand their full meaning. To me, when taken in connection with other expressions used by our Saviour concerning himself, they convey an idea of mystery, of union with God inexplicably close; a mystery into which we can but imperfectly penetrate, because it is but imperfectly revealed. But at the same time, while the expression conveys the idea of an unknown exaltation, it distinctly implies derivation and dependence. If words mean any thing, — if we are to use them according to their intelligible meaning, — the Son owes his existence to the Father, and cannot therefore be self-existent. The very idea of sonship is of derivation, and is therefore inconsistent with the doctrine both of identity and of equality. If words mean any thing, he who is the Son of the living or supreme God cannot be himself the supreme God, but must be derived from him, and dependent on him.

In the statement now given, I have expressed my whole belief concerning Christ. In the words of Peter, I say, "He is the Christ, the Son of the living God." With that confession of faith Jesus was satisfied; for he said, "Blessed art thou, Simon, son of Jonah, for flesh and blood hath not revealed it unto thee, but my Father which is in heaven." It is, then, not only the opinion of the Apostles, confirmed by Christ, but it is also the direct inspiration of the Father in heaven. We have reason, therefore, to be satisfied with it. We adopt it, word for word, as the confession of faith in this church, and are willing to receive no other. It constitutes us Unitarians. My task this evening is to show its meaning more fully, and to prove that it is taught, not only in the words of the text, but everywhere else in the Bible.

First of all, you will observe, and I call your attention particularly to it, that those who accuse us of believing that Christ is a mere man, are in error. They are prejudiced or misinformed. If by a mere man they mean one like ourselves, or like the prophets of the olden time, Moses, or Isaiah, or Ezekiel, or John the Baptist, the charge is entirely untrue. I know of no Unitarians who hold such a belief. There may be individuals who receive it, as there are individuals in the Presbyterian Church who believe in infant damnation; but I hope they are few in both cases. You will also find, among nominal Unitarians, some who have almost no faith at all; who hold to Jesus only as they might hold to Socrates. I pass no sentence upon them, for it is not our part to sit in judgment or to pronounce anathemas; but I do say, that they are not to be taken as the exponents of the Unitarian faith. I feel satisfied, from observation which has been very extended, that there is no denomination in which Christ is more heartily received than in our own. A vulgar prejudice has been sometimes excited against us, by calling Unitarianism the half-way house to infidelity; but I believe that it has been the means of saving more persons from infidelity than any other form of belief. It addresses itself to thinking men and encourages them to think independently, but it does not make shipwreck of faith. It receives Christ as the divine master and guide, but at the same time proves his doctrines to be consistent with enlightened reason.

Unitarians, as a body of believers, everywhere, agree in the belief that Christ is the special messenger of God; that his mission was divine; that his character was sinless; that his authority was so directly from God, that whatever he taught is the teaching of the Father. "For he spake not of himself, but as the Father gave him commandment, so he taught." He was divine, therefore, in his mission, in his character, and in his authority. This is not the description of a mere man. Consider only the distinction of absolute freedom from sin, to say nothing of his superhuman wisdom and power; how completely does that distinction alone place him by himself! What nearness to God does it give him! We can but imperfectly conceive it. Our own sinfulness is so great, it is so inherent in our nature so inseparable from the development of our thoughts and affections, that we but imperfectly understand its debasing influence. I believe that, if we could this day be absolutely freed from sin, we should be lost in amazement at the height to which we would rise, and the comparative degradation in which we now stand. To be absolutely freed from sin, is to be indeed the Son of God; it is the highest moral exaltation; and when we add thereto such authority and power as belonged to Jesus, we see how very far he is from all our ideas of a mere man.

Upon one point of considerable importance, Unitarian believers are divided in opinion. Some of them, among whom are included a majority of English Unitarians, believe that the existence of Christ began when he was born at Bethlehem of Judea. They defend this belief by the records of his life, from his infancy to his crucifixion.— That he calls himself a man, and is so called and so treated by his disciples; and that he was subject to the wants, to the infirmities, the sufferings, and death, which belong to humanity. This class of believers is sometimes called Humanitarian. Although there are many arguments difficult to answer, by which their belief is sustained, I have never been satisfied with it. I do not now belong, and I never have belonged, to their number. We acknowledge them as brethren, and among them we see many of the most excellent names which adorn the Unitarian calendar; but I cannot agree with them in opinion. I admit, however, that the most essential point in the Christian faith is, not the time when Christ's existence began, nor the metaphysical elements of his nature, but the degree of his authority to speak in the name of God. If the Scriptures say truly, that to him the Spirit was given without measure, and that he has power to give eternal life to whom he will, this alone is enough to make his religion divine, and to enable us to receive him as our Saviour.

The other part of Unitarians believe that Christ came down from heaven to accomplish his work on earth; that from his dwelling in the bosom of the Father, he was sent, a willing messenger, to bring glad tidings of great joy, and to accomplish, for our salvation, a work which we could not do for ourselves. To this faith I give my adherence, and more strongly, from year to year, as I become more thoroughly acquainted with the Bible. As I have already said, I do not pretend to define it exactly. The nature of his being, before he came upon earth, is entirely unknown to us. The degree of his nearness to God, either then or now, we can but imperfectly understand. But I am unable to interpret his language concerning himself, or the language of his Apostles concerning him, consistently with any other belief.

When the Jews were objecting to him his youth and the obscurity of his birth, he answered, John viii. 56 "Your father Abraham rejoiced to see my day, and he saw and was glad. Then said the Jews unto him, thou art not fifty years old, and hast thou seen Abraham? And Jesus said unto them, before Abraham was, I am." In his prayer to the Father, he says, John xvii. 5, " Glorify thou me with thy own self, with the glory which I had with thee before the world was." And again, verse 24, " For thou lovedst me before the foundation of the world." At another time, when the Jews objected to his saying that he was the bread which came down from heaven, he said to his disciples, John vi. 61, " Doth this offend you? What and if ye shall see the Son of man ascend up where he was before ?" John the Baptist, in speaking of him, said, John i. 30, " After me cometh a man which is preferred before me, for he was before me."

"In this connection let me quote the Saviour's words. ' No man hath ascended up to heaven but he that came down from heaven.' Is it said that coming down from heaven simply implies a divine commission ? Why, then, did not John the Baptist, who certainly had a commission, no less from God than that of Jesus, speak of himself as coming down from heaven? But he in this same chapter (John iii.) expressly speaks of Christ as coming down from heaven in a sense in which he himself did not come from heaven, and of himself as being of the earth in a sense in which Christ was not of the earth. ' He must increase,' says the Baptist, ' but I must decrease. He that cometh from above is above all. He that cometh from the earth is earthly, and speaketh of the earth. He that cometh from heaven is above all.' " *

In accordance with this view, it is said of Christ, " He made himself of no reputation"; which means, literally, he divested himself, as if of what he had previously possessed or enjoyed, " and took upon him the form of a servant, and was made in the likeness of men, and being found in fashion as a man, he humbled himself." (Phil. ii. 7.) In another place it is said, " Ye know the grace of

---

* Peabody's Lectures.

our Lord Jesus Christ, that though he was rich, yet for your sakes he became poor, that ye, through his poverty might become rich"; by which we understand that Jesus for man's salvation, passed from a richer to a poorer, from a more lofty to a more humble condition.

It is true that Christ is called a man; but properly considered, this is no objection to the view now offered. The essential idea of humanity is not derived from weakness and sin, but from that mysterious connection of the soul and body, — the immortal spirit with the corruptible flesh, — by which the soul is made subject to earthly influence. Our spiritual nature is probably the same, in its elements, with that of the most exalted archangel. The highest created spirit, therefore, if clothed in human form and subjected to human sympathies and temptations, would become, properly speaking, a man. Consider the distance between different members of the human family, as at present constituted. Take Newton, with his mind reaching up to the heights of heaven, and place him by the side of one of those thousands of his own countrymen, whose thoughts have scarcely a larger range than that of a brute; see how wide a field is covered by that word, man! For these two are brothers, of the same family, of the same descent. And so, as Jesus is called "the Son of God," and we also are honored by the same name, — as he is called the "firstborn of every creature," with reference to that spiritual family of which we are the younger children, — I believe that we may claim kindred with him. Coming from the bosom of the Father, to make known the Father's love, he took our nature upon him. He became a man. The attributes of humanity belonged to him. Suffering as we suffer, tempted in all points as we are, yet without sin, "he gave us a perfect example in the performance of those duties which are incumbent on all created spirits, and which are the same to all, namely, love and obedience to the great father-spirit, love and charity to all fellow-spirits." He was a man, more perfectly than any other. In him humanity was glorified; the ideal, which is proposed to us all was perfected in him. The weakness of the flesh was not only brought into subjection to the spirit, but the spirit was made stronger through the victory, as it is written, Christ "was made perfect through suffering." All human passions, all desires, all purposes, were thus made pure and heavenly; and thus it is that through his humiliation "God has highly exalted him, and given him a name above every name."

It will be seen, therefore, that those passages of the Bible which speak of the great exaltation of Jesus cannot be brought against us, as Unitarians, unless they distinctly imply his equality with the Father. This needs to be carefully remarked. Trinitarians are apt to think that every text which speaks of Christ's great power, and wisdom and authority, or of his exaltation at the right hand of God militates against our doctrine; but it is not so. He is to us also, the Son of the living God, the image of the Father through whom, both in his person and in his life and in his words, as much is made known of the Infinite God as it is possible for us to know in our present state. There is but one way to overthrow the Unitarian doctrine. It is to prove not that Christ is "a Prince and a Saviour by the right hand of God highly exalted," but that he is the Infinite God himself, by whom that exaltation was given. It is not to prove that the Father made himself manifest through the Son, as it is written, "the word was made flesh," that is, "the divine wisdom and power were manifested in a human form," but it is to prove that the Father, who is the being manifested, is the same with the Son, who was the medium of the manifestation. The question between us and Trinitarians is simply this: Did the Saviour, when he said, "My Father is greater than I," mean what he seemed to say, and what he was understood by those who heard him to say, or did he mean that, while there was an apparent inferiority, he was in fact equal with the Father, possessed of the same attributes, being himself the absolute and Supreme God?

Here is the true point of the controversy. I think that it settles itself. I scarcely know how to bring any arguments to make it plainer. I am almost afraid that in multiplying words, in so plain a case, I may darken counsel, but must try. I shall show you, first, that Christ himself distinctly denies the possession of divine attributes; secondly, that the Apostles, when they speak of him in the highest terms of exaltation, and therefore of his highest nature, uniformly declare his entire dependence on God, the Father.

The leading attributes of Deity are Self-existence, Omnipotence, Omniscience, and Infinite Goodness. If we can prove by the words of Christ himself that he denies the possession of one and all of these, I think our case is made out. His distinct denial of any one of these attributes would be enough; but, in fact, he denies them all.

1. Of Self-existence. This attribute implies absolute independence; an existence to which no other being is necessary; self-derived and self-sustained. But Christ declares a hundred times that he came not of himself, but that the Father sent him; see John viii. 42, "Neither came I of myself, but he sent me." He declared that he was indebted to the Father for the support of his existence, John vi. 57, "As the living Father hath sent me, and I

live by the Father"; and again, John v. 26, "As the Father hath life in himself, *so hath he given* to the Son to have life in himself. I can of mine own self do nothing; as I hear I judge, and my judgment is just, because I seek not mine own will, but the will of the Father who sent me." He says also, John x. 18, "No man taketh my life from me, but I lay it down of myself; I have power [the literal meaning is *authority*] to lay it down, and I have authority to take it again; *this commandment have I received* of my Father." Which also agrees with 2 Cor. xiii. 4, "Though he was crucified through weakness, yet he liveth by the power of God." Here is a distinct and full denial of underived and independent existence. Upon the authority of Christ himself, therefore, we say that he was not the Self-existent God.

2. Omnipotence. Jesus distinctly and repeatedly declares that he is not in possession of this attribute. He uniformly speaks of his power as being given by the Father and exercised under his direction. But the idea of omnipotence is inconsistent with that of derived power and delegated authority. Omnipotence cannot be given by one to another. In such a case he who gives must be greater than he who receives. Therefore, when the Saviour says, Matt. xxviii. 18, "All power is given to me by the Father," the word *given* necessarily limits the word *all*. The text is sometimes quoted to prove Christ's omnipotence, but we think it proves just the contrary. Again he says, John v. 19, "The Son can do nothing of himself"; and again, verse 30, "I can of mine own self do nothing." And still more pointedly, when he was asked for a certain distinction by James and John, he answered Matt. xx. 23, "To sit on my right hand and on my left is not mine to give; but it shall be given to them for whom it

is prepared of my Father." In his last conversation with his disciples he says, "If ye loved me, ye would rejoice, because I said, I go unto the Father; for my Father is greater than I." (John xiv. 28.) These declarations are distinct and unqualified. We are therefore ready to receive Christ in the highest exaltation which the Scripture accords to him. But we feel at the same time compelled to believe his own words. These are the best authority. They do not teach us that he is Almighty, but that he is dependent in all things upon the Father.

3. Omniscience. This is the attribute by which he who possesses it knows all things. An omniscient being needs not to be instructed. Thus it is written of the Almighty, Isaiah xl. 13, " Who hath directed the spirit of the Lord, or, being his counsellor, hath taught him? With whom took he counsel, and who instructed him, and taught him in the path of judgment, and taught him knowledge?" Compare those words with the words of the Saviour, John vii. 16, " My doctrine is not mine, but his that sent me "; and xiv. 24, " The word which ye hear is not mine, but the Father's who sent me." And again, viii. 28, " As my Father hath taught me, I speak these things." And even more strongly, xii. 49, " I have not spoken of myself, but the Father who sent me, he gave me a commandment, what I should say and what I should speak. Whatsoever I speak, therefore, even as the Father said unto me, so I speak " All this is an expression of imparted knowledge, which, however great it may be, must always be less than omniscience. And accordingly we find, Matthew xxiv. 36, and Mark xiii. 32, when asked concerning a future event, Jesus answered, " Of that day and that hour knoweth no man ; no, not the angels in heaven, neither the Son, but the Father." In Matthew it says, " but my Father *only.* '

We cannot escape from these words if we would. We place implicit reliance upon whatever Christ taught. We believe that God spake through him; and upon his own authority we say, that omniscience is the attribute of the Father only.

4. Infinite Goodness. We believe that Christ was perfectly free from sin, that he went about doing good, and finished the work which God gave him to do. In this sense therefore, he was perfect; but there is a sense in which none but an Infinite being is good, and *in this sense* Christ denied it of himself, Mark x. 18. When some one called him " Good Master," he answered, " Why callest thou me good? there is none good but one, that is God." The same words are found in the parallel passages in Matthew and Luke.

What are we to say of these plain denials by the Saviour himself, not of one only, but of all these attributes? We have his own words to prove that he is neither Self-existent, Omniscient, All-wise, nor Infinitely Good. On what ground can we set aside his testimony? We shall be told, perhaps, that all this is spoken only of his *human nature;* that he denied these attributes as a man, although he was conscious of possessing them as God.

We find no fault with those who are satisfied with this answer, but it does not satisfy us. It does not seem to us the fair interpretation of plain language. For, first, we find no passage in the Bible, and there is none, in which it is taught that our Saviour had two natures, one human and one divine; but he is always spoken of as a single being " the Christ, the Son of the living God." And secondly we think that when he spoke of himself without qualification, using the personal pronouns, *I*, and *myself*, and *me*, he must have used them in their common meaning, and he was certainly, at the time, so understood. If he had intended to have been understood differently, he would have given some indication of it. As he gave none, we take his words in their plain and obvious meaning. Just as you would understand me, if I were to say, "I do not know such a thing," or "I cannot do such a thing," without qualifying the words, so do we understand him. We dare not understand him otherwise. For would it be right for me to say, "I do not know such a thing," if I really know it? and defend myself by saying, that my body does not know it, but my mind does? or that I know it as a clergyman, but not as a citizen? Such would not be a fair use of language; and if the Scripture were to be interpreted in such a manner, there is absolutely no doctrine which could not be proved from it. We understand Jesus simply as he spoke, and therefore, while we pray for the time when "at the name of Jesus every knee shall bow, and every tongue confess him to be the Lord," we remember that this must always be done "to the glory of God the Father."

The quotation of this verse brings us to the last topic of my present discourse. I am still to prove that the Apostles, in those passages where they speak of Christ's highest exaltation, uniformly declare that he is dependent for all upon the Father. For this purpose I shall use only those texts which are commonly considered proofs of his Supreme Divinity. They are therefore undoubtedly applicable to his highest nature, whatever they may be; and if, when so spoken of, his dependence on God is alleged, our argument will be conclusive. For, as I have already said, we do not pretend to define the degree of exaltation which belongs to Christ. We remain Unitarians so long as we believe that the Father alone is the Supreme God.

1. There is probably no text oftener quoted against us, than the first part of the Epistle to the Hebrews, particularly the eighth verse: "But unto the Son he saith, Thy throne, O God, is for ever and ever; a sceptre of righteousness is the sceptre of thy kingdom; thou hast loved righteousness and hated iniquity." The word God is here applied to Christ, and is understood as a proof of his deity. This, however, would be an uncertain proof, for the same word is applied quite frequently in a subordinate sense. It was applied to Moses, who was said to be "a god to Pharaoh." Exod. vii. 1. Those also were called Gods to whom the word of God came. See John x. 35. We must look, therefore, to the connection to see what its meaning is, in this case; and we read directly after the words quoted, "Therefore God, even thy God, hath anointed thee with the oil of gladness above thy fellows." Observe, therefore, which is the point of our argument in this case, that, even when spoken of as God, there is the Supreme God over him, from whom he receives his anointing, and by whom he is raised above his equals. Let me read to you, also, the beginning of that same chapter, that you may see how plainly the dependence of Christ upon the Father is expressed.

"God, who at sundry times and in divers manners spake in time past unto the fathers by the prophets, hath in these last days spoken unto us by his Son, whom he hath appointed heir of all things, by whom also he made the worlds; who being the brightness of his glory, and the express image of his person, and upholding all things by the word of his power, when he had by himself purged our sins, sat down on the right hand of the Majesty on high being made so much better than the angels, as he hath by inheritance obtained a more excellent name than they

For unto which of the angels said he at any time, Thou art my Son, this day have I begotten thee? And again, I will be to him a Father, and he shall be to me a Son." We admit that words cannot easily express higher exaltation than this. It was the Apostle's intention to speak in the strongest terms which were consistent with truth, and he has done so. In reading them we perceive that the exaltation of Christ is greater than we can fully comprehend. But at the same time we perceive, with equal plainness, delegated authority and absolute dependence on the Father. On the one hand, we can have no doubt that his highest nature is here spoken of, for there is no passage in which stronger words are used. On the other hand, we read that he did not speak of himself, but that God spoke by him; that in all his highest offices he was the agent of God, working only by God's power; that he obtained a more excellent name than the angels by inheritance, according to the appointment of God; that there was a time when his existence began, as plainly expressed in these words, "*This day* have I begotten thee." In the tenth, eleventh, and twelfth verses, which are a quotation from Psalm cii., the Almighty himself is addressed as the source of all power and might; after which the Apostle returns to his former subject, the dignity of Christ, which he again ascribes to God as the Author and Giver.

We refer next to the Epistle to the Colossians, the first and second chapters. I cannot quote them at large, but request you to read them carefully for yourselves. You will find the same remarks hold good which have been made on the passage already quoted. You will find language which you cannot reconcile with the doctrine of mere humanity; you will feel amazed, as in the presence of a being highly exalted above every one of us; but every where you will find proof of *derived* authori.y and *dependent* existence. He is "the image of the invisible God," and therefore not the invisible God himself. He is "the first-born of every creature," and therefore himself a created being The reason and the source of his great exaltation are distinctly given : " For it pleased the Father that in him all fulness should dwell."

In both of these passages language is used which seems to imply that Christ is the agent by whom all things were created and upheld. I think that this properly refers to the spiritual world in heaven and on earth, of which he is appointed the head and director; but time will not allow me to consider this question now. It is altogether unimportant to our present argument, for it does not affect the real exaltation of Christ, nor does it alter the fact of his complete dependence on the Father.

We next refer to Phil. ii. 5, 11; in the sixth verse it is said of Jesus Christ, "Who, being in the form of God, thought it not robbery to be equal with God"; of which Calvin says, "The form of God here signifies majesty; I acknowledge, indeed, that Paul does not make mention of Christ's divine essence." To be in the form of God means, to be the image or manifestation of God; which is also the interpretation adopted by Le Clerc and Macknight. The proper meaning of the words, "Thought it not robbery to be equal with God," is that given by Bishop Sherlock, namely, "He was not tenacious of appearing as God; did not eagerly insist to be equal with God." This is the meaning adopted by Coleridge, Professor Stuart, Luther, Melancthon, Archbishop Tillotson, Paley, and many others of the most eminent Trinitarian writers. But the exact meaning of the words is not important to our present argument Whatever they mean, their limitation is found in the ninth and following verses. "*Wherefore God hath highly exalted him,* and given him a name which is above every name, that at the name of Jesus every knee shall bow, of those in heaven, and those in earth and those under the earth, and that every tongue should confess that Jesus Christ is the Lord, to the glory of God the Father."

One of the most important books in the New Testament, in a doctrinal point of view, is the Acts of the Apostles. It contains their first preaching after they had been fully instructed in their work. Whatever they knew of Jesus or believed concerning him will undoubtedly be found there. They were impelled at the same time by strong affection for their master, by a deep sense of their former unfaithfulness to him, and by the direct command of God, to declare the whole truth. Now what is the substance of their preaching? Read the first ten chapters of that book and determine. I think that you will agree with me that it is a series of Unitarian discourses. There is not an expression, not a single word that I cannot use, or that I am not accustomed to use as a Unitarian believer. They indeed declare that Christ is a Prince and a Saviour, that he is both Lord and Christ; but how is it that he obtained this authority? Let them answer in their own words: "Therefore let all the house of Israel know assuredly that *God hath made that same Jesus whom ye have crucified both Lord and Christ.*" Acts ii. 36. "Then Peter and the other Apostles answered and said, We ought to obey God rather than men. The God of our fathers raised up Jesus, whom ye slew and hanged on a tree. *Him hath God exalted* with his own right hand, to be a Prince and a Saviour, to give repentance to Israel and forgiveness of sins." Acts v. 29. This is the utmost of their preaching; further than this they never go; and thus far we as Unitarians go with them

These Scriptures all of them speak of Christ in his highest nature. You hear them quoted every day to prove his absolute deity. Yet you perceive that all of them, by showing his dependence on God the Father, prove the exact contrary, and teach that though so highly exalted, even above our perfect comprehension, he is not the Supreme God nor equal to God the Father. In further explanation of this view I will quote the following passage from the First Epistle to the Corinthians, xv. 24–28; which is a distinct and full declaration of the Unitarian doctrine:—
" Then cometh the end, when he shall have delivered up the kingdom to God, even the Father, when he shall have put down all rule and all authority and power. For he must reign till he hath put all enemies under his feet. The last enemy that shall be destroyed is death. For he hath put all things under his feet. But when he saith, All things are put under him, it is manifest that he is excepted who did put all things under him. And when all things shall be subdued unto him, then shall the Son also himself be subject unto him that put all things under him, that God may be all in all."

I cannot express my faith as a Unitarian in plainer words than these. They are a brief statement, in the most unequivocal terms, of the general, pervading doctrine of the Bible. Such is the testimony of Christ concerning himself, and such the testimony of the Apostles concerning him as their Lord and Master. It is all consistent with the Saviour's own prayer to the Father, " That they might know Thee, the Only True God, and Jesus Christ whom thou hast sent"; and with the words of Paul, " To us there is but one God, even the Father, and one Lord Jesus Christ."

There are, however, a few texts which, taken by themselves, are thought to teach a different doctrine. Among these the introduction to the Gospel of John is the most important. I wish to examine them fairly and carefully, and must therefore defer them to another evening. In the mean time, and in conclusion, let me again say that, with the plain words of Christ and his Apostles to guide us, we ought not to be troubled or shaken in our faith by a few comparatively obscure and difficult passages. In so large a subject we ought to expect some remaining difficulties, and we have reason to thank God that the general doctrine of the Bible is so plainly taught, that he who runs **may read.**

OUR LORD JESUS CHRIST.

TO THE LAW AND TO THE TESTIMONY. — Isaiah viii. 20.

I HAVE promised this evening to explain the principal texts in the Bible, which are supposed to militate against the Unitarian doctrine. The task is by no means easy; not because there is inherent difficulty in any of such texts, or in all of them put together, but because the work, to be thoroughly done, would be very tedious. A single passage, if at all obscure, may require a great many words in its critical exposition. Nor is the hearer always able to decide whether the explanation is satisfactory or not; he must take a great part of the critical statements upon authority, and he is very apt to be suspicious of unfair dealing, when an interpretation is given to familiar words different from that to which he is accustomed. He is apt to think that the language, instead of being explained, is explained away. For this reason, I am accustomed, in explaining a disputed passage, to give "Orthodox" Trinitarian authority for the explanation which I adopt. It is not because I think that such testimony is more respectable than that of our own writers, but because I would put the explanations given beyond the suspicion of unfairness. For if, with reference o any particular text, we can show that eminent scholars in the Trinitarian ranks have given the same explanation, although they have thereby weakened their own argument, it will follow that the words are fairly susceptible of such a meaning. In adopting a Unitarian explanation, upon Trinitarian authority, we need have no fear that the words are distorted, or the meaning perverted, merely to suit our end.

Now it is a very singular fact, and it is one which greatly confirms me in my Unitarian belief, that there is not a single text in the Bible with regard to which we cannot bring good Trinitarian authority for its Unitarian meaning; or in other words, there is not a single text which is not abandoned by one or more of the most celebrated Trinitarian theologians. I repeat that this gives me great confidence in our interpretations of the Bible. We might otherwise fear that our interpretations were made to suit ourselves,— we might suspect ourselves of unfairness.

After all, however, the explanation which we adopt of particular disputed passages should be to a great extent determined by the general view which we take of the Scripture doctrine. When a text is ambiguous, that is, when it may be explained in accordance either with the Trinitarian or Unitarian belief, we should be guided in our choice of the two explanations by the general meaning of the whole Bible. It would not be right to set aside a doctrine which is acknowledged to be that of a whole book, because there are a few sentences which will bear a different construction. Before proceeding, therefore, to the examination of the texts in question, let me again remind you of the great strength of argument by which the Unitarian doctrine concerning God and our Lord Jesus Christ has been proved to be the general and prevailing doctrine of the Bible. Let me remind you that the Old Testament not only declares the Unity of God, but that the express object of the dispensation under Moses and the Prophets was to establish that doctrine in the world; that it was taught without any qualification, and received by the Jews just as we receive it; that when Christ came, he reaffirmed the doctrine, using the same words which had been spoken from Mount Sinai, without the leas hint that they were to be understood in a different manner but, on the contrary, declaring in so many words, that the Father is the only true God; that the Apostles took up the same instruction, teaching that the God of Abraham, and of Isaac, and of Jacob, "the God of their fathers," was also the God and Father of our Lord Jesus Christ.

I think that it will not be disputed that this is the general instruction of the Bible. If we are to modify this instruction, it must be because the texts which we are this evening to examine require it; but if it can be shown that every one of them can be explained, and has been explained, even by Trinitarians themselves, in accordance with the general doctrine as above stated, we shall be justified, I think, in adopting such explanation, and thereby putting our minds at rest.

1. First, we will examine several of those texts in which peculiar names are given to Jesus Christ, of which the principal are Isa. ix. 6, Jer. xxiii. 5, 6, and Matt. i. 23. In these passages the names "Wonderful, Counsellor, the mighty God, the everlasting Father, the Prince of Peace," "Jehovah our righteousness," and "Immanuel, or God with us," are applied to Christ, and there are no passages more relied upon to prove his supreme divinity. To understand them, we must have some knowledge of the Scripture usage, in the application of such names to remarkable persons or places. By which we shall learn,

that the use of such names proves nothing of the nature of the person to whom they are given, but that they are only descriptive of some circumstances attending his birth, or the offices he is expected to fill.

Nothing is more common in the Bible than such descriptive names as the following. An altar was called by Jacob " El-Elohe-Israel," — God, the God of Israel ; another by Moses, " Jehovah-Nissi," — Jehovah, my banner. The place where God provided the ram instead of Isaac is called " Jehovah-Jireh," — God will see or provide. In the same manner, the names of many distinguished persons in the Old Testament, if translated into English, have similar meanings, and, without a knowledge of this Hebrew custom, would convey very false ideas. Elias means " my God," and you will remember that when our Saviour, on the cross, cried out, " Eloi, Eloi," &c., those who stood near thought that he was calling upon Elias. Elijah means, literally, " my God Jehovah," and Zedekiah, " the righteousness of Jehovah." Gabriel means, literally, " the strength of God," or " the strong God," and it is worthy of remark that the Hebrew words comprising the name are identically the same as those which, in the text before us, are translated " the mighty God," — GIBOR AEL. We are accustomed to these names, and, as they are not translated in their ordinary use, we do not think of their literal meaning; but when just such names are applied to Christ, they are translated into English, and insisted upon as a literal proof of his divine nature. Whereas, properly considered, they prove nothing upon the subject either one way or the other.

We proceed now to a particular examination of the texts in question. Isa. ix. 6 : Of which we remark, first, that the words were originally spoken, not of Christ, but of

King Hezekiah. The distinguished Hugo Grotius, and Samuel White, fellow of Trinity College, Cambridge, both of them Trinitarians, take this view of it. The words of the latter are as follows: "The government shall be upon his shoulders; that is, that he, King Hezekiah, shall reign in the throne of David, as the metaphor signifies, and as the prophet more fully explains himself in the following verse; which cannot be literally true of our Saviour, whose kingdom was not of this world, as David's was; but in a *second* and *sublimer* sense the expression denotes that power which God devolved on his Son, of governing his spiritual kingdom, the Church." Now we argue, that, whatever the names may indicate, if in their primary application they were given to King Hezekiah, they cannot in their secondary application to Christ prove his Supreme Divinity. In the phrase " the mighty God," the word translated " God" means, literally, strong. And we may therefore read " Mighty Potentate," if we prefer. The definite article also is wanting in the Hebrew, so that it would be, A mighty God or Potentate. This is the interpretation which Martin Luther gave, and he declares that the epithet " belongs not to the person of Christ, but to his work and office." Rosenmuller, one of the most learned Orthodox commentators, says: " It is evident that AEL denotes strong, powerful, and is used in Ezekiel xxxi. 11 of King Nebuchadnezzar, who is called AEL GOYIM, ' the mighty one of the heathen,' or, if AEL means God, ' the God of the heathen.' "

The phrase " the everlasting Father" can scarcely be applied to Christ in a literal sense, according to the Trinitarian system; for this would confound the distinction between the Father and the Son. Accordingly we find that Calvin and Grotius translate the words " the Father of the age," or dispensation. Bishop Lowth, Carlile (in his work

"Jesus Christ the Great God our Saviour"), and Dr. Adam Clarke translate it, "Father of the everlasting age," and in the same manner a great many other Orthodox writers. Such a rendering we are willing to accept, together with the meaning which Calvin gave to the words, namely, "He who is always producing new offspring in the Church." But we prefer the explanation of Dr. Wells, of the Church of England, who says that, when Christ is called the everlasting Father, it means that he is the "author of our eternal salvation, and the Father or head of the world to come, that is, of the Gospel state." I will also add the testimony of Luther, who says that the title Everlasting Father denotes not a person, but his work, and that the Hebrew particle translated "everlasting" does not properly signify eternal, but of indefinite continuance.

We next refer to Jer. xxiii. 6, in which Christ is called "Jehovah our righteousness"; but it so happens that in chapter xxxiii. 16 of the same prophet, exactly the same name is applied to the city of Jerusalem. "In those days shall Judah be saved and Jerusalem dwell safely, and this is the name wherewith she shall be called, — Jehovah our righteousness." So that we have no difficulty in either case. Le Clerc explains the passage for us as follows: "The Messiah is said to be called Jehovah our righteousness to denote that in his days, and by his means, God would, in a remarkable manner, exhibit proofs of his own justice by punishing the wicked and defending the righteous; so in chapter xxxiii. 16, Jerusalem is designated by the same title, meaning that God would cause righteousness to flourish in that city, namely, in the Christian Church."

In Matt. i. 23 it is written, "They shall call his name Immanuel, which, being interpreted, is God with us." The words are a quotation of a prophecy from Isa. vii. 14, of which Professor Stuart, of Andover, says: " Originally and literally it is applicable only to the birth of a child within a period of three years from the time when the prophecy was spoken; for how could the birth of Jesus, which happened seven hundred and forty-two years afterwards, be a sign to Ahaz that within three years his kingdom was to be freed from his enemies? Such a child, it would seem, was born at that time; for in chapter viii. he is twice referred to, as if then present, or at least then living." That the application of the prophecy to Christ proves nothing concerning his nature, I could bring abundant Trinitarian testimony, but content myself with that of the eminent man just now quoted. In his reply to Dr. Channing, he says: " What you say respecting the argument concerning Christ's divine nature, from the name given him in Matt. i. 23, accords in the main with my views. To maintain that the name Immanuel proves the doctrine in question is a fallacious argument, although many Trinitarians have urged it. Jerusalem is called Jehovah our righteousness. Is Jerusalem therefore divine?" I have been more careful in explaining these passages, because the same explanation will apply to other texts, in which similar names are given to Jesus Christ.

2. An argument is drawn for the Supreme Divinity of Christ, from the fact that similar language is sometimes applied to him and to God. The answer in all such cases is, that in its application to God we understand it in its highest sense; but to Christ only in that sense which belongs to him as the Son of God. Thus it it is said, " I am Jehovah, and beside me there is no Saviour." Yet Christ is called our Saviour. Jehovah is called the Redeemer of Israel, and Christ is also called a Redeemer. Such language gives us no trouble. In the highest sense, all salvation, all help

all guidance, and all support come from God. He alone is the author and giver of every good gift, and thus, in the ascription of praise, we say, " To the only wise God, our Saviour." But Jesus Christ is also in a true and real sense our Saviour, our guide, our supporter, our Redeemer. Not by his independent power, indeed, but because, Acts v. 31, " God hath exalted him with his right hand to be a Prince and a Saviour, to give repentance to Israel, and forgiveness of sins." In the same manner, many things are said to be done by God which are also said to be done by Christ ; as, that God will judge the world, and also that Christ is the judge of all. But this is explained when we are taught, Acts xxii. 31, " That God will judge the world in righteousness by that man whom he hath ordained "; and so in all other instances of the same sort. Christ acts as the agent, the representative, the messenger of God, but we ascribe the work to him, always remembering, however, that he does not speak of himself. John vii. 16, 18. To the same effect I will quote the following very clear language of Professor Stuart : " Nothing can be more erroneous in most cases, than to draw the conclusion that, because the Scripture asserts some particular thing to have been done by God, therefore he did it immediately, and no instruments were employed by him. In interpreting the principles of human laws, we say, ' He who does any thing by another does it himself.' Does not common sense approve of this, as applied to the language of the Scripture ? Nothing can be more evident than that the sacred writers have expressed themselves in a manner which recognizes this principle."

On the same principle we explain those passages which teach us to " honor the Son as we honor the Father," and that " he who denieth the Son denieth the Father also." For in all such cases the ambassador and the king, the principal and the agent, God and his Christ, are one; and accordingly Christ himself said, "He that receiveth you receiveth me, and he that receiveth me receiveth him that sent me."

In further application of the same principle, it is said in Isaiah and Malachi, "The voice of him that crieth in the wilderness, Prepare ye the way of the Lord, make his paths straight"; and again, "Behold I send my messenger before my face"; which words in Matt. iii. 3 are applied to the coming of John the Baptist to prepare the way for Jesus Christ; for the coming of Christ as the messenger of God was the coming of God himself to bestow the blessings of a new revelation. If you will keep this rule of interpretation in your mind, namely, that the same language will often be applied directly to the principal and also to the agent, because whatever the agent does the principal may be said to do, it will remove much of the obscurity of the sacred writings.

3. There are a number of instances in the New Testament in which Christ is said to have been worshipped, either by his disciples or other persons. For instance, Matt. xxviii. 9, when, after his resurrection, his disciples "came and held him by the feet and worshipped him"; and verse 17, "When they saw him they worshipped him." Upon this passage Dr. Adam Clarke, the great Methodist commentator, remarks as follows: "This kind of reverence is in daily use among the Hindoos; when a disciple meets a public guide in the streets, he prostrates himself before him, and, taking the dust from his teacher's feet, rubs it on his forehead, breast," &c. And Dr. J. P. Smith, an equally good authority, says: "The prostrate position, which denoted the highest reverence and respect, is manifestly described, but the expression does not necessarily import more than the

men, exalted kind of civil homage." In fact, the word "worshipped" is very frequently used to signify respect and homage, and so it is used in application to temporal rulers; see Matt. xviii. 26, in the parable of the creditor who took his servant by the throat, saying, Pay me that thou owest. "The servant therefore fell down and worshipped him, saying, Lord, have patience with me and I will pay thee all." Also see Luke xiv. 10 : "Then shalt thou have worship in the presence of those who sit at meat with thee." We must, therefore, in all cases determine by the circumstances the nature of the worship given; but with regard to the highest or religious worship, we have the command of Jesus himself, "Thou shalt worship the Lord thy God and him only shalt thou serve." Matt. iv. 10. I will remark that the word here translated *serve*, whenever it occurs, means religious worship such as we give to God only, and there is *no case* of its application to Jesus Christ.

There are two texts in which it is supposed that direct prayer is offered to Christ. The first is Acts vii. 59, at the martyrdom of Stephen : "And they stoned Stephen, calling upon God, and saying, Lord Jesus, receive my spirit!" By turning to your Bibles, you will see that the word *God* is printed in italics, from which we know that it is not in the original, but supplied by the translators. We may read, therefore, calling upon *Christ*, or simply "calling out." Now we are to remember that Stephen is represented as seeing Jesus at the right hand of God, and his exclamation was like an appeal made to one who was present. But apart from this, there is nothing in the words of Stephen which every believer in Christ may not adopt in his dying hour. Our brightest hope of heaven is to be with him, and the natural aspiration of our hearts will be, when the time of our departure comes, that he may receive us into his fold and acknowledge us as his brethren. No one is more heartily Unitarian than I am, but I think that such words would come to my lips as the natural prompting of my heart. So have I often heard the dying Christian, with heaven already opening to his eyes, whisper the name of parent or child, or some dear friend long since departed as if communion with the dead were already begun. How much more may we thus speak the name of Jesus with whom the spiritual bond is closest of all, whose intercession with the Father is for us, and who hath gone before to the blessed mansions, to prepare a place for us, that where he is we may be also! It was only yesterday that I stood by the bedside of a dying friend, who, wearied with her long-continued suffering, exclaimed, "O, how I long to go home! O that Jesus would take me to himself!" Yet her belief is as decidedly Unitarian as my own.

Another instance of what is thought to be direct prayer to Jesus Christ is found 2 Cor. xii. 8: "For this thing I besought the Lord thrice, that it might depart from me; and he said unto me, My grace is sufficient for thee, for my strength is made perfect in weakness; most gladly therefore will I rather glory in my infirmities, that the power of Christ may rest upon me." Dr. Hammond of the English Church interprets this as a prayer to God. But I think that the connection shows it to have been Christ whom Paul addressed. It is not, however, what we commonly call prayer, but a personal request to his master. For he has been giving us an account of Christ's appearing to him in a vision, by a special revelation, and in that vision, with Christ present before him, he makes the petition here recorded. It cannot therefore be considered as an authority for prayer to Christ, under ordinary circumstances. Our proper and only sufficient authority upon this subject is in the words of Jesus Christ himself, who says, speaking of the time when he should no longer be on earth, John xvi. 23, "In that day ye shall ask me nothing; verily, verily, I say unto you, whatsoever ye shall ask the Father in my name, he will give it you; hitherto have ye asked nothing in my name; ask and ye shall receive, that your joy may be full."

This is the Christian doctrine of prayer. We pray to God the Father only, but we pray through Jesus Christ, or in his name; that is, as his followers and disciples, who believe in his words, who trust in his promises, who receive the benefit of his life, his suffering, and death, who look to him as our advocate with the Father, and who receive through him, as the mediator between God and us and as the living head of his Church, the spiritual blessings which are needed to sustain our souls: further than this the Scriptures do not authorize us to go.

The frequent ascriptions of praise and honor to Christ give us no trouble. To him, in fact, under God, we owe all our spiritual blessings; and so long as we keep it distinctly in mind, that all should be done to the glory of God the Father, the ultimate source of all blessing, we may properly ascribe " blessing and honor and glory and power," not only 'to Him who sitteth upon the throne, but to the Lamb for ever." Rev. v. 13. You will observe in the words just quoted, and almost everywhere else in the book of Revelation, how clearly the distinction is kept up between God and Christ; between him who sits upon the throne, and the Lamb. Read the whole of the fifth chapter and it will appear still more plainly. There is no book of the New Testament which offers so great difficulties in its interpretation as that to which I now refer. It is written in the highest strain of poetry and prophetic imagery, and no two writers can be found who agree as to its exact meaning. I think therefore, that it ought not to be used as a principal authority upon disputed points of doctrine.

If it is true (which we consider by no means certain) that it is Jesus who says, Rev. i. 11, "I am Alpha and Omega," its explanation is difficult; for we can scarcely understand how such words are applicable to any one but the Almighty. But the difficulty is at once increased and removed, when we find the words used by one who commanded John not to worship him: "See thou do it not; for I am thy fellow-servant; worship God"; for it was the same person who used these words who said directly after, "I am Alpha and Omega; the beginning and the end; the first and the last." Rev. xxii. 8, 13. I can understand such language only by supposing that Jesus and also the angel were speaking in the name of God. In the same manner Moses says, Deut. xxix. 2, 6, "I have led you forty years in the wilderness; . . . . . that ye may know that I am the Lord your God." See also Deut. xi. 13 – 15. In both of these passages Moses used language, which, if it had been used by Christ, would be stronger in proving his Deity than any now quoted for that purpose. We should not, therefore, attach so great importance to isolated and obscure texts. I am persuaded that it is better to look to the plainer books of Scripture for our chief instruction.

4. The strongest support of the Trinitarian doctrine concerning Christ, and, as it appears to most readers, the greatest difficulty in the way of Unitarians, is found in the introduction to the Gospel of John; to which I now ask your attention for a few minutes. It is an obscure and difficult passage of Scripture. But its obscurity arises, chiefly, from our failing to consider the object which the Apostle had in view, and the circumstances under which he wrote. Upon

these it chiefly depends what meaning shall be given to the word Logos, and therefore to the whole passage in question. It is commonly supposed that his object was to declare that Jesus Christ was God, the second person of the Trinity. The Logos is taken as another term for Christ, as if the Apostle had said, " In the beginning was Jesus Christ, and Jesus Christ was with God, and Jesus Christ was God."

This explanation is thought by those who receive it to remove all difficulty, and to make the whole passage plain. But it is only because they are accustomed to it, and do not perceive the force of the words used. In fact it expresses a direct contradiction, which cannot itself be explained, except by saying that the terms used have no distinct or intelligible meaning. When we say that James is *with* John, we cannot take a plainer way of saying that James and John are two separate beings. To say that James is *with* John and that James *is* John, is a contradiction in terms. Why does not the same hold true of God and of Christ? If by the Logos we understand a personal existence distinct from God, we may say that the Logos was with God, but not at the same time that the Logos was God. To say one is to deny the other. We shall not, therefore, escape the difficulty of the passage by adopting the Trinitarian theory. We may not be quite satisfied with our own explanation, and some parts of it may continue to perplex us, but we cannot receive an explanation which so evidently contradicts itself.

Secondly, we cannot adopt it, because it also contradicts the Apostle's repeated assertions concerning Christ, and his plain statement of the object with which his Gospel was written. There is none of the Gospels which is so full in its declarations that Christ is the *son* of God, not God himself, and it is in this Gospel that we find ecord of Christ's most distinct denial of the Divine attributes. At its close, the Apostle informs us what his general purpose had been, as follows (John xx. 31): "These are written that ye might believe that Jesus is the Christ, the Son of God, and that, believing, ye might have life through his name." Would he have so stated his purpose, if his real object had been to prove that Christ was himself the Infinite God, whose Son he declares him to be, and by whom he was anointed? Let me also remind you of his words, in this same first chapter which is supposed to teach that Christ is God: "No man hath seen God at any time; the only-begotten Son, who is in the bosom of the Father, he hath declared him." This is the true doctrine, in accordance with which we should explain the introductory sentences now under consideration.

Let us look, next, at the literal meaning of the Greek word Logos. There is no word in English which exactly answers to it. In Latin, it was sometimes translated *ratio*, or reason, sometimes *verbum*, a word, or *sermo*, a discourse. The connection alone must determine, in each case, which of these meanings should be used. In the present case, if we translate it by *ratio*, reason, it would mean the Divine Mind or the Wisdom of God. Tertullian, one of the Christian Fathers, whose authority as a learned man is very high, understood it in this way.* The same meaning was adopted by Le Clerc and by Dr. Wall, both of them Trinitarians, and no Greek scholar will deny that such a translation of the word Logos is strictly correct. If we prefer it, therefore, or if we think that this meaning suits the connection, we are at liberty to adopt it. We have no objection, however, to the translation which is given in the English Bible,

---

* Tertullian. advers. Praxeam, Cap. 5.

if it is rightly considered; for by the Word of God we can understand nothing else but God's power and wisdom, and it is but another expression for the Divine Mind, the Spirit of God, or God himself. So when we read in the book of Psalms, that " by the Word of Jehovah the heavens were made, and all the host of them by the breath of his mouth," it is only another mode of saying that these things were done by the power and wisdom of God, or by God himself. It is precisely this which the Apostle John asserts in the first verses of his Gospel; namely, the Word of God, considered as creating and upholding, is only another expression for God himself.

But why did the Apostle think it necessary to make a formal statement of a truth, so plain that it is almost self-evident? and how do we account for the peculiar phraseology which he used? In these questions consists the whole difficulty of the case, and we can answer them only by referring to the times when the Apostle wrote and the particular doctrines which he intended to combat.

There is a natural tendency in the human mind to draw a veil between itself and God. Our faculties are so limited, and the idea of an Infinite and Omnipresent Being, who does all things by his own direct power, is so far above our comprehension, that we often use words that imply an intermediate agency, even when we know that they are only a different way of saying the same thing. Thus we speak of Nature, of Providence, of the Laws of God, the Spirit and the Word of God, almost as if they were agents through whom God acts, instead of different names or expressions for the ever-present God himself. We are not deceived by such terms, and although they sometimes have the effect of removing God farther from us, they are undoubtedly an aid to our feebleness. But in ancient times, when the education of the religious world was more imperfect, and especially among the Oriental nations, where imagination gives so strong a bias to all intellectual development, such words very often come to be realities. The Wisdom, Reason, and Understanding of God, his Spirit, his Word, came to be considered as real agencies, and in the progress of time as personal existences, indistinctly defined, but real and living. Hence arose serious and fatal errors. Such ideas, incorporated into the Christian system, made it little better than a modified form of polytheism. The God in whom we live and move and have our being, of whom and by whom and through whom are all things, was no longer preached, and an incomprehensible jargon, of Emanations and Æons and the like, was substituted; a perversion of Gospel truth little better than its rejection.

What I am now stating is an historical fact. By referring to any good Ecclesiastical History of the first and second centuries, you will learn that a system of philosophy, such as I have described, originated with Philo, an Alexandrian Jew, a man of great learning, whose influence spread itself through all the learned world of his age. Many of his disciples became converts to Christianity, and from them arose the sect of the Gnostics, one of the most influential but pestilent heresies of the early Christian Church. They had their origin in Apostolical times, although their system was not completely matured until later. Their head-quarters were in the city of Ephesus, where, according to the uniform testimony of antiquity, the Gospel of John was written. It is very difficult to learn exactly what they taught, but it was something like the following:—

"They maintained that the Supreme God dwelt in the remote heavens, surrounded by chosen spirits, *Æons* as they called them, and gave himself very little concern with what took place upon earth; that the world was created by an inferior and an imperfect being, who was also the author of the Jewish dispensation; that Christ was sent by the Supreme God to deliver men from the tyranny of this Creator, and from the yoke of his law; that there were also various created spirits, or Æons, sustaining different offices, independently, for the most part, of the Supreme Deity; the names of some of which Æons were Life, Light, and particularly the Logos, which represented the Divine Reason or Wisdom; and that the Æon Light became incarnate in John the Baptist. All these spiritual existences were represented as distinct from each other and from the Supreme God." *

The existence of such a system at the time when John wrote, and among the very people whom he was seeking to convert, or who had been already converted to Christ, would justify us in supposing that the introduction to his Gospel, which is so exactly suited to the purpose, was in fact intended for its overthrow. But the evidence is made complete by the testimony of Irenæus, a competent and unimpeachable witness. He lived in the early part of the second century, and was a friend and pupil of Polycarp, who was a personal friend of John himself. In his work against heresy, he says that the beloved disciple wrote his Gospel for the express purpose of refuting the false and absurd notions which the Gnostics were beginning to spread in Asia Minor.

---

* **Peabody's Lectures.**

With these historical facts to guide us, we can without difficulty learn the meaning of this famous passage. It teaches that the Logos, the Word or Wisdom of God, which the philosophical Christians thought to be an emanation from God and a personal existence separate from him, was only another name for God himself. It never had a personal existence separate from God, but from the beginning was with God and was God. (For we may properly say that wisdom is *with* God and that God *is* wisdom.) By him, that is, by the Logos of God, or by God himself, — for the grammatical construction admits of either meaning, and both are in fact the same, — by him all things were made. From him Life and Light proceed to enlighten every one who comes into the world. He sent John, not as an Æon called Light, but as a witness of Him who was the true Light. And the Logos, the Wisdom or the Word of God, which is God himself, became flesh; God was made manifest in man, namely, in Jesus Christ, who dwelt among us, and we beheld his glory, as of the only-begotten Son of God, full of grace and truth.

This is the substance of the Apostle's meaning. It is suited to the purpose he had in view, and it agrees with the doctrine of his whole Gospel. I do not pretend to remove all obscurity from the passage, but I have no doubt that this is, substantially, its correct interpretation. We understand it as an assertion of the absolute unity of God, of his direct agency in all things, and of the divine mission of our Lord Jesus Christ. It therefore confirms our belief in Him "who is the only true God, and in Jesus Christ whom he hath sent."

5. The words contained in John x. 30 are much relied upon to prove the Deity of Christ: "I and my Father

are one." We interpret the words as meaning unity in counsel, design, and power, not unity of substance. I have before me not less than twenty Trinitarian authorities to confirm this view, from which I select the words of Calvin and of Professor Stuart, because their names are most familiar to you. No one will suspect either of them of leaning to the Unitarian side of the question.

"In the present case it seems to me that the meaning of 'I and my Father are one' is simply, I and my Father are united in counsel, design, and power. So in John xvii. 20, Christ prays that all who shall believe on him 'may be one, as thou Father art in me and I in thee; so they also may be one in us.' See also Gal. iii. 28, and 1 Cor. iii. 8."— *Professor Stuart, Answer to Channing.*

6. 1 John v. 20: "And we know that the Son of God is come, and hath given us an understanding that we may know Him that is true; and we are in Him that is true, *even* in his Son Jesus Christ. This is the true God and eternal life." The word *even* you will find in italics, and may therefore omit it and read, "We are in Him that is true, in his Son Jesus Christ." Of which expression Calvin says, that "the Apostle intends to express the means of our union with God, as if he had said, that we are in God by Christ." Erasmus, Archbishop Tillotson, Adam Clarke, and others, interpret it in the same way. Dr. Bloomfield even more plainly: "We are in union with the true God by means of his Son Jesus Christ." The words, "this is the true God," may grammatically refer either to Christ, or to "Him that is true." We refer it, of course, to God the Father, who is the chief subject of discourse. In which construction we have the authority of Erasmus

Grotius, Rosenmüller, and others. The language of Grotius is as follows: —

"This is the true God; namely, he and none else whom Jesus hath declared to be the object of worship. The pronoun *outos*, this, not unfrequently relates to a remote antecedent; as in Acts vii. 19; x. 6. 'And eternal life'; this is said by metonymy. The Apostle means that God is the primary and chief author of eternal life. So also Christ is called Life, John xi. 25; xiv. 6, because, next to God the Father, he is the cause of eternal life."

7. Zech. xiii. 7, "Awake, O sword, against my shepherd and against the man that is my fellow, saith Jehovah of hosts." Here it is argued, that Christ is spoken of as the fellow or equal of God. But in fact, the literal meaning of the word translated *fellow* is "one with me," or near me, and implies no equality at all. As to the meaning of the word, there is no dispute among critics. But as the passage is quoted with a great deal of confidence in many Trinitarian pulpits, it may be worth while to read the remarks of Calvin upon it. "The word translated *fellow* means an associate, a neighbor, or a friend, and whoever is joined to us in authority. I have no doubt that by this title God distinguishes his shepherds, because he represented himself by them to his people. The prophet speaks of shepherds as God's associates, on account of their union with him, and because, as St. Paul says, they are fellow workers and laborers together with God."

8. Much reliance is placed on the exclamation of Thomas John xx. 28, "And Thomas answered and said unto him My Lord and my God." I am not sure what explanation of these words is the true one. They were not spoken as a confession of faith, as the words of Peter were, when

asked by Christ, "Whom do ye say that I am?" but they were spoken by the most sceptical of all the Apostles, under the influence of the most profound astonishment. But I am quite sure that they are not a declaration that Christ is the Supreme God, for this simple reason: that, even if such a doctrine be true, neither Thomas nor any other of the twelve had any knowledge of it at the time. "It may be justly doubted," says Dr. Bloomfield, Bishop of London, "whether the so lately incredulous, because prejudiced and unenlightened disciple, had then, or at any time before the illumination of the Holy Spirit at Pentecost, any complete notion of the divine nature of Jesus as forming part of the Godhead." Indeed, it can be clearly proved, and is admitted by a great many Trinitarian writers, that the Apostles had no conception of Christ's deity when Thomas spoke. I therefore adopt the opinion of the celebrated Kuinoel, whose commentary on the Scriptures is a standard work in Orthodox universities, and who says, that, if the words are addressed to Jesus, "Thomas used the word God in the sense in which it is applied to kings and judges (who are considered as representatives of Deity) and pre-eminently to the Messiah."

9. We next refer to Romans ix. 5, "Whose are the fathers, and of whom, as concerning the flesh, Christ came, who is over all, God blessed for ever. Amen." The whole argument against us in this passage depends on the punctuation. You know that the original manuscripts of the New Testament are without any punctuation. The sentences are not divided from each other by any marks, and translators are obliged to punctuate as they think the sense requires. Now in this case, if we adopt the punctuation proposed by Griesbach, or that by Rosenmüller

both of them Trinitarians and eminent in learning, the sense is materially changed. Let the period be placed after the word *all*, and it then reads, " Of whom, as concerning the flesh, Christ came, who is over all. God be blessed for ever." Which words are added as a doxology by the Apostle, in the way in which, in several instances, he has inserted a doxology in the midst of a paragraph.

10. In Acts xx. 28, we read, " Feed the Church of God, which he hath purchased with his own blood." The true reading of this passage is the " blood of the Lord"; but I do not care to insist upon this. The expression is of course to be understood figuratively. No one will contend that it was literally the blood of God. It can mean nothing else than that God purchased the Church with the blood of his own Son Jesus Christ, which, on account of his intimate union with the Father, may be figuratively called God's own blood. This is the meaning which is adopted by the celebrated Baxter, author of the Saints' Rest.

11. John xiv. 9, " He that hath seen me hath seen the Father, and how sayest thou then, Show us the Father." The meaning of these words is sufficiently explained by the connection in which they stand. If you will read the fourteenth chapter through, they will give you no trouble Christ made a clear revelation of God, and therefore made known of the Father as much as it is possible for us at present to know. So the words are explained by Dr William Sherlock: " He that hath seen me hath seen the Father, that is, in plain words, the will of God was fully declared to the world by Christ. Thus God was seen in Christ." It is but another mode of saying that God was **made manifest** in Christ,— which leads me to speak of

another text, 1 Tim. iii. 16, which expresses the same doctrine: "And without controversy great is the mystery of godliness; God was manifest in the flesh, justified in the spirit, seen of angels, preached unto the Gentiles, received up into glory." It needs no explanation to the Unitarian believer, for that God was manifest in Christ, and that thus the Wisdom of God, or his Word, was made flesh, we strongly maintain. For although "no man hath at any time seen God himself, yet the only-begotten Son hath declared him." The essential difference still remains between God, who is manifested, and Christ, by whom the manifestation is made.

We have now examined the most important texts which are supposed to be at variance with the Unitarian belief. If I have omitted any, they are such, I think, as are sufficiently explained by the connection in which they stand. For we again say, the highest terms of exaltation applied to Christ give us no trouble, so long as the connection shows that he received his exaltation, "because it pleased the Father that in him all fulness should dwell." We may be at a loss to define the degree of his authority, but one such expression as that proves, beyond all doubt, that his authority was not independent or supreme.

As to the greater part of these texts, I feel sure that our explanation is good and sufficient. In a few cases only it remains doubtful whether the Unitarian or Trinitarian explanation is the most natural. But even if there were a great many such cases, the weight of evidence which has been adduced from the general testimony of the Bible is enough to decide us. For my own part, my mind rests upon this subject without any doubt or wavering, for to me the meaning of the Bible seems so plain, that if there were fifty texts which I could not perfectly understand, although I should feel the difficulty, they would not shake my faith.

ARGUMENT FROM HISTORY

WHOSE ARE THE FATHERS. — Romans ix. 5.

My object this evening is to show the argument for the Unitarian doctrine derived from Ecclesiastical History.

It is a subject to which more importance is attached than it really deserves. For, as we have the Bible in our own hands, we can read the words of Jesus and of his Apostles for ourselves, and these alone are enough to form our faith. They are indeed the only conclusive authority. To Jesus the Holy Spirit was given without measure. Whatever he declared himself to be, therefore, we are bound to believe; neither more nor less. Show us that he laid claim to be the Infinite and Supreme God, and we will so receive him; but as we can find no such words from his lips, but, on the contrary, repeated and distinct declarations of his entire dependence on God the Father, we receive this doctrine, and shall hold to it, let those who are called the Christian Fathers teach what they may. We do not, therefore, regard the subject of this evening as essential to our general argument. It becomes important chiefly because of the stress laid upon it by others.

By the Roman Catholics, the early traditions of the Christian Church and the writings of the Christian Fathers are regarded as the strong bulwarks of their faith. They do not hesitate to admit that the leading doctrines of Christianity cannot be proved by the Bible alone. Let me quote some of their language to this effect. "We believe the doctrine of a triune God," says Cardinal Hosius, "because we have received it by tradition, though not mentioned at all in Scripture." — Conf. Cathol. Fidei, Chap XXVII.

"Those who bind themselves to Scripture alone, and who do not set up any other rule of law or belief, labor to no purpose, and are conquered by their own weapons, as often as they join battle with such pests [the Unitarians], that conceal and defend themselves likewise with the language of Scripture alone. And we know from history, that this frequently happened to them in the conferences and disputes into which they entered with the Photinians and the Arians." — Petavius, De Trin. Lib. III. Cap. xi. 9; Theol. Dog., Vol. II. p. 301.

"That the Son is of the same essence as the Father, or consubstantial with him, is not manifest in any part of sacred Scripture, either in express words, or by certain and immutable deduction. These and other opinions of the Protestants no one can prove from the sacred writings, the traditionary word of God being laid aside. This request has often been made, but no one has made it good. Scripture itself would, in many places, have seemed to exhibit the opposite doctrine, unless the Church had taught us otherwise." — Masenius, Apud Sandium, pp. 9 – 11.

To the same purport I might quote many other Roman Catholic authorities. "It is also a remarkable fact, that the

Roman Catholic has often triumphed over his Protestant antagonist by demonstrating that the great principle of Protestantism, the right of individuals to interpret Scripture without resting on tradition and the authority of the Church, inevitably leads to Unitarianism."

Protestant believers in the Trinity will not of course go so far as this, but even among them concessions have been made of almost equal importance. Many of their best writers, as Hooker, Bishop Beveridge, Bishop Smallridge, and even Carlile (author of the work " Jesus Christ, the great God our Saviour "), and many others, admit that the doctrine of the Trinity is not " directly and explicitly declared, but a doctrine of inference, which ought not to be placed on a footing of equality with a doctrine of direct and explicit revelation." — Carlile, pp. 81, 369.

I do not know whether to quote the Oxford tracts, which were written by Newman, Pusey, and others before they became Roman Catholics, as Catholic or Protestant authorities. Newman was certainly a nominal Protestant when he wrote the following words: " The most accurate consideration of the subject will lead us to acquiesce in the statement, as a general truth, that the doctrines in question have never been learned merely from Scripture ; surely the sacred volume was never intended, and was not adapted, to teach our creed." (Newman, Arians of the Fourth Century p. 55, quoted in Wiseman's Lectures, p. 93.) You may say, that, although a Protestant, he was on the high-road to Catholicism and should not be quoted as a Protestant authority; but I think that this was one thing that made him a Roman Catholic, namely, that he was not able to prove the doctrines of his Church by the Bible alone ; and therefore, appealing to the authority of the Church in their defence, he came upon Catholic ground, and step by s.ep travelled from Oxford to Rome, almost before he was aware of the inevitable result. For I believe it is strictly true, that the doctrines of the Church of England, and of the "Orthodox" Church generally, upon the subject we are now discussing, cannot be consistently held by those who admit the exclusive authority of the Scriptures, and the right of private judgment.

In some shape or other the authority of the Church or of tradition, or of the catechism or creed or prayer-book, must be brought in, or the doctrines themselves will soon be abandoned.

From considerations such as these, great importance is attached to the Christian Fathers. Many persons, who are really in doubt whether the doctrine of the Trinity is taught in the Bible, are held in its belief because they suppose that it has been the doctrine of the Church from the very beginning, and therefore must have been taught by the Apostles; and probably the same opinion is a source of difficulty to many Unitarians. For if it were true, that that doctrine was taught in the first two or three centuries, as it is taught now, we might have some trouble in accounting for it. It would have been very strange for such a doctrine to have grown up all at once, if not derived from the Apostles themselves.

I shall therefore attempt to show, and think that I shall succeed in showing, that the departure from the Unitarian or Evangelical faith was very gradual, and that the doctrine of the Trinity as now taught was not established in the Christian Church until the last part of the fourth and beginning of the fifth centuries. This I shall do, first, by two arguments of a general nature;

and secondly by quotations from the Christian Fathers themselves.

1. In the early ages of the Church we find mention of two sects, the Ebionites and Nazarenes. They are sometimes called " Judaizing Christians," because they adhered, the former strictly, and the latter more loosely, to the Mosaic law. The Ebionites believed that Christ was a mere man, and were always reckoned among the heretics by orthodox believers. The Nazarenes " believed in the miraculous birth of Christ, and that he was in some way united with the Divine nature; they refused to discard the ceremonies prescribed by Moses, but did not obtrude them upon the Gentile Christians. They, moreover, rejected the additions to the Mosaic ritual made by the doctors of the law and by the Pharisees." This sect WAS NEVER COUNTED AMONG THE HERETICS in the first three centuries. Mosheim informs us that " Epiphanius, a writer of the fourth century, of no great fidelity or accuracy of judgment, was the first who branded them as heretics."* But these Nazarenes were Unitarians, beyond all doubt, — and would they have escaped the brand of heresy, if the majority of believers had been Trinitarians?

What I have now said is upon the authority of Mosheim and Neander, both of them Trinitarian writers of high repute. My own belief is, that the Nazarenes were the primitive Christians, converts from Judaism, who retained a little too much of their Jewish predilections, just as the Apostle Peter did in his early ministry. But in other respects they were primitive Gospel Christians. I think so, partly because they were in such good repute in the Christian world

---

* Mosheim, Eccl. Hist., Book I. Cent. 2, Part 2, Chap 5, § 2, note 3

that even their Judaizing tendencies did not separate them from the orthodox communion, and partly because their name is that which was given (at first by way of reproach) to all the disciples of Christ, because he was a citizen of Nazareth. Acts xxiv. 5.

Secondly. We derive a second general proof from Ecclesiastical History in the creeds or confessions of faith used in the first four centuries. By their examination, we shall find there was a gradual departure from the simplicity that is in Christ, and an equal departure from the Unitarian belief. The confession of faith used by the Apostles themselves, as recorded in the book of Acts, was very brief and simple. "I believe that Jesus Christ is the Son of God." Acts viii. 37. This creed was the rock on which our Saviour assured Peter that he would build his Church. Matt. xvi. 16. It was this which the Apostle Peter taught to the assembled Jews on the day of Pentecost. Acts ii. 36. The Apostle John wrote his Gospel for the special purpose of inculcating it. John xx. 31. And when Paul was miraculously converted to a knowledge of the truth, the great burden of his preaching was, to convince his hearers of the same. Acts ix. 22.

When converts were made from among the heathens, another article was necessarily added, expressive of the belief in One God, even the Father. Hence was formed, with some further additions, what is called the Apostles' Creed. It was not written by the Apostles themselves, but it was in general use in the first three centuries, and was regarded as containing the whole apostolical faith. Now we contend that it is nothing more or less than a Unitarian creed. We can adopt it, word for word without any explanation : —

"I believe in God the Father Almighty, and in Jesus Christ, his only Son, our Lord; who was, by the Holy Spirit, born of the Virgin Mary; under Pontius Pilate he was crucified and buried; the third day he rose from the dead; he ascended into heaven and sitteth on the right hand of the Father; from thence he shall come to judge the quick and the dead. I believe in the Holy Spirit; the holy Church: the forgiveness of sins; the resurrection of the body, and life everlasting."

This is the exact form in which the creed was used in the second, third, and fourth centuries, and it was considered the sufficient rule of faith in the Church until the year 325. I think that it would not have been regarded as sufficient if the Trinitarian belief had generally prevailed. It would not be regarded alone as sufficient in the present day. It would not be considered safe in the Episcopal and Roman Catholic Churches to discard the Nicene and Athanasian Creeds and to retain this as the only confession of faith; nor in the Presbyterian Church would it be considered safe to adopt it, instead of the Assembly's Catechism. But it satisfies us, as Unitarians, and if we thought it right to use any confession of faith, other than the New Testament itself, I know of none which we could adopt more heartily than this which is called the Apostles' Creed.

As corruptions of doctrine prevailed more and more, the Apostles' Creed was found to be insufficient. At the Council of Nice, A. D. 325, another creed was established. It was adopted against great opposition, although the whole authority of the Emperor Constantine was exerted, and it was more than fifty years before it was firmly established in the Church; so reluctantly did the Christian world depart from its first formulas of faith. It is also to be especially remarked, that the Nicene Creed, as at first adopted, does not teach the doctrine of the Trinity, for it says nothing of the personality of the Holy Spirit. Nor does it teach the absolute equality of Christ with the Father, although it uses unscriptural language, such as a Unitarian cannot adopt. The idea of derivation of the Son from the Father is still retained. He is the *Son* of God, the *begotten* of the Father, God OF God, — that is, *derived* from God, not absolutely God in the same sense with the Father. If you will examine the history of the Council of Nice, you will find that this is the meaning then attached to the words.*

The first creed in which the Trinitarian faith is stated as now received, is the Athanasian Creed. It was not composed by Athanasius, but by some unknown author in the fifth century. It is such a creed as was needed in the Church, after it had completely abandoned the Unitarian faith; and it is a strong argument in our favor, that no such creed is to be found until the fifth century, a time when corruptions of every sort abounded. You will thus perceive how gradually the transition was made, step by step, and "as the first creed is avowedly the one held by Unitarians, and the last one held by the Trinitarians, the inference is irresistible, that the Church, which was Unitarian in the beginning, gradually became Trinitarian."

2. Having given these two general arguments, from undisputed facts in the history of the Church, I now proceed to give several quotations from the early Fathers. Among those of the highest authority, and whose names will be familiar to you, are Justin the Martyr, Irenæus, Clemen' of Rome, Clemens Alexandrinus, Origen, and Eusebius

---

* See Mosheim's Ecclesiastical History.

These are the most highly esteemed of the Christian Fathers before the Council of Nice, and they all concur in giving Unitarian testimony.

CLEMENT OF ROME, a personal friend of Paul, mentioned in the Epistle to the Philippians, (Phil. iv. 3,) calls Jesus " the sceptre of the majesty of God "; and we find near the close of his Letter to the Corinthians the following doxology, which is such as a Unitarian would have written : — " Now God, the inspector of all things, the Father of all spirits, and the Lord of all flesh, who has chosen our Lord Jesus Christ, and us by him to be his peculiar people, grant to every soul of man that calleth upon His great and holy name, faith, fear, peace, long-suffering, patience, temperance, holiness, and sobriety, unto all well pleasing in his sight, through our high priest and protector Christ Jesus, by whom be glory and majesty and power and honor unto Him now and for ever." Again he says, " Have we not all one God, and one Christ, and one spirit of grace poured upon us all ? " which is exactly the language of the Apostle Paul himself, with whom he was contemporary.

JUSTIN MARTYR, who addressed a defence of Christianity to Antoninus Pius, about the year 140, was among the first to use that language concerning Christ which afterwards grew into the doctrine of his supreme divinity and holds a high rank among the Orthodox Fathers; he has this language concerning Christ : — " 'The Father is the author to him, both of his existence and of his being powerful and of his being Lord and God." You will observe that Christ is here called God, but the connection shows that it is in a subordinate sense. In another place he says, " He was subordinate to the Father, and a minister to his will."

IRENÆUS, who wrote a large work upon the subject of heresies, A. D. 172, says: "All the Evangelists have delivered to us the doctrine of one God and one Christ, the Son of God"; invoking the Father, he calls him "the *only* God," and according to several of the most considerable of the early Christian writers, a common epithet by which the Father is distinguished from the Son is, that he alone is *Autotheos*, or God of himself.

CLEMENS ALEXANDRINUS calls the Father alone "without beginning," and immediately after characterizes the Son as "the beginning and the first-fruits of things, from whom we must learn the Father of all." He also says, "The Mediator performs the will of the Father; the word is the Mediator, being common to both, the seal of God, and the Saviour of men, God's servant, and our instructor."

TERTULLIAN expressly says, "That God was not always a Father or a Judge; since he could not be a Father before he had a son, nor a Judge before there was sin, and there was a time, when both sin, and the Son, which made God to be a Judge and a Father, *were not*."

ORIGEN, the most learned of the Fathers, wrote about the year 225; he says, "The Father only is 'the Good,' and the Saviour, as he is the image of the invisible God, so is he the image of his goodness." Again he says, "If we know what prayer is, we must not pray to any created being, not to Christ himself, but only to God the Father of all, to whom our Saviour himself prayed." "We are not to pray to a brother, who has the same father with ourselves; Jesus himself saying, that we must pray to the Father, through the Son." Yet this same Origen frequently calls Christ God, although in a subordinate sense. For when accused of believing in two Gods, he explained himself as follows: — "He who is God *of himself* is The God; for which reason he says in his prayer to the Father, that they may know Thee the only true God; but whatever is God besides him, (who is so of himself,) being God only by a communication of his divinity, cannot so properly be called The God, but rather A God," or Divine.

Such language is very common until the beginning of the fifth century; and whenever Christ is called God before that time, the word is to be understood in the sense in which Origen used it. Thus ARNOBIUS says, "Christ, a God under the form of a man, speaking by the order of the principal God." Again, "Then at length did God Almighty, the only God, send Christ." And LACTANTIUS says, "Christ taught that there is one God, and that he alone ought to be worshipped; neither did he ever call himself God; because he would not have been true to his trust, if, being sent to take away Gods and assert One, he had introduced another besides that one. Because he assumed nothing at all to himself, he received the dignity of perpetual Priest, the honor of Sovereign King, the power of a Judge, and the name of God."

I shall quote but one other authority, EUSEBIUS, the father of ecclesiastical history, who wrote about the year 320. He says, "There is one God and the only-begotten comes from him." "Christ being neither the Supreme God, nor an angel, is of a middle nature between them; and being neither the Supreme God nor a man, but a Mediator, is in the middle between them, the only-begotten Son of God." "Christ the only-begotten Son of God, and the first-born of every creature, teaches us to call his Father the true God, and commands us to worship him only"

These quotations are, I think, plain and conclusive. I might multiply them to a great extent, if needful. But these are enough for our present purpose, which is to show that the changes in Christianity were very gradual, from the plain and intelligible doctrine taught by Christ and his Apostles, to the difficult and unscriptural doctrines of the Athanasian Creed.

The chief source of these changes or corruptions was the Platonic philosophy. Justin Martyr, Tertullian, and nearly all of the early Christian Fathers, were Platonists before they were Christians. They brought into their new religion as much of their old philosophy as they could. They thus ingrafted many ideas borrowed from Plotinus, Porphyry, Proclus, and other Platonists of that age; and what was equally bad, they applied Platonic language to the expression of their Christian faith, by which great confusion of ideas was introduced. Among the terms thus borrowed was the Greek word Trias, used by the Platonic philosophers to express some subtile distinction in the divine nature usually called the Platonic trinity. It was not a distinction of persons properly so called, nor is it easy to say exactly what it did mean. The word was first introduced into the discussion of the Godhead among Christians by Theophilus of Antioch, in the second century, and was afterwards used by Origen in the third century. It was translated into the Latin by Tertullian, about the year 200, by the word Trinitas, of which the English word Trinity is the exact translation. Many other words in the newly invented phraseology came from the same source, and many peculiar ideas concerning the Logos, or Word of God. I shall not trace them now; but to show the extent to which "Orthodox" Christians of later times, when the

Trinity was becoming established, considered themselves indebted to the Platonic philosophy, I will quote one sentence from the celebrated Augustine. He says, that he " was in the dark with regard to the Trinity until he found the true doctrine concerning the divine word, in a Latin translation of some Platonic writings, which the Providence of God had thrown in his way."

I do not suppose that any one will accuse me of intentional unfairness, in the representation now made of the Christian Fathers. I have not claimed any one of them as being what we would call a sound Unitarian. The best of them used language and inculcated ideas which came from the Platonic school quite as much as from Christ. All that I contend for is this: that the farther we go back, the nearer we come to the true doctrine which is life eternal, namely, "to know the Father, the only true God, and Jesus Christ whom he has sent." There is no proof whatever, that what is now called the doctrine of the Trinity was in existence before the Council of Nice. To this effect I will quote the authority of George Christian Knapp an eminent Trinitarian writer, whose "Lectures on Christian Theology," as translated by Leonard Woods, Jr., are a standard work with Trinitarian believers. After a full and learned discussion of the whole subject, he distinctly admits that it is "impossible to prove the agreement of the earliest Christian writers with the common Orthodox doctrine as established in the fourth century." Vol. I. pp. 294, 299, &c.

Again he says, "It is obvious, that the *Unity*, of which these philosophical Fathers speak, is nothing more than *unanimity*, agreement, correspondence in feelings, consent in will, in power, and in the application of power to particilar objects. They do not mean by the use of the word to signify that the Son and Holy Spirit were God, in the full meaning of the word, and in the same sense in which the Father is God. In short, these philosophical Christians asserted rather the *divineness* of the Son and the Spirit, and their divine origin, than their equal deity with the Father. Thus it is obvious, that they entertained far different views of the Divinity of the Son and Spirit, of which they often speak, than we do at the present time." "Indeed, the belief in the subordination of the Son to the Father, for which Arianism was the later name, was commonly adopted by most of those Fathers of the second and third centuries, who assented in general to the philosophy of Plato. And had not Divine Providence interposed in a special manner, there is reason to think it would have been the established doctrine of the Church." And again, " With regard to the Holy Spirit more particularly, we may remark that, during the three first centuries of the Christian era there was nothing decided by ecclesiastical authority respecting his nature, the characteristics of his person, or his relation to the Father and the Son. Nor was any thing more definite established at the Council of Nice. To believe in the Holy Spirit was all that was required." — *Ib.* p. 313.

Such is the fact concerning the Fathers of the first three centuries. The writer just quoted accounts for it, being himself a Trinitarian, by saying that the true doctrine was corrupted by the infusion of the Platonic ideas. But if that true doctrine had been the Trinity, we should find it more distinctly stated the farther we go back in the record; of which the exact contrary is true. The earliest writers are the most distinctly Unitarian, and in proportion as the

Platonic philosophy came in, there was a gradual, but rapid departure from the truth, until, after long and violent struggles, the Christian world settled down into the Athanasian Creed. It was undoubtedly by the permission of Divine Providence, but it was through the direct influence of the civil power, and the result of the most terrible persecutions.

From that time until the sixteenth century, comparative darkness was over the face of the Christian world. But no sooner was the light of the Reformation kindled, than the Unitarian doctrine again appeared. Resisted alike by Catholic and Protestant, it was held at the peril of a man's life; yet many were found to profess it. In Geneva, Michael Servetus was burned to death, at the instigation and by the authority of Calvin, who thereby gave another proof that " the blood of the martyr is the seed of the Church," for Geneva is now one of the strongholds of the Unitarian faith.

We might name many others, in Germany, in France, and in England, who bore a like testimony; for from that time to this our faith has never been without its martyrs and faithful confessors. Nor have we any reason to be ashamed of those who have borne our name. They have been comparatively few, for the doctrine has been unpopular and opposed by all the strength of the Christian world. But although until modern times they were few in number, they have been great in intellect, profound in learning, and eminent in piety. John Milton, England's great poet; Sir Isaac Newton, her greatest philosopher; John Locke, her profoundest metaphysician; Nathaniel Lardner, author of the most learned work on Christian evidences ever written,— were all of them close students of the Scripture, and all of them believers in the Divine Unity as we receive it. Ever

Dr. Isaac Watts, whose hymns are the music of every church, became in the last years of his life a Unitarian. If great names could support a cause, these would do it. We might add to them many others of the living and the dead, equally good. But we do not rely on such arguments. We appeal to the Sacred Scriptures alone, to the glorious company of the Apostles and to Christ their living head. Yet surely we may be pardoned, when we hear our Church vilified and ourselves excluded from the Christian communion, if we remind our opponents that so many of the names of which Christendom is most proud are found in the Unitarian ranks.

In the present day, we have every reason to be satisfied with the progress of our faith. It is extending itself far more rapidly than most persons are aware; not only by the growth of Unitarian societies, so called, but by the diffusion of Unitarian ideas everywhere. So far as they are true, we hope that they will continue to prevail more and more. If they are untrue, if they are a perversion of God's word, we hope that they may soon pass away. If we hold error, we do so ignorantly, for we honestly believe that we hold the truth as it is in Jesus.

I will therefore close this sermon in the words, almost the dying words, of Dr. Watts, in his solemn address to the Deity. As sincere inquirers after Scriptural truth, we may adopt them as our own.

"Dear and blessed God! hadst thou been pleased, in any ore plain Scripture, to have informed me which of the different opinions about the Holy Trinity, among the contending parties of Christians, had been true, thou knowest with how much zeal, satisfaction, and joy, my unbiassed heart would have opened itself to receive and embrace the divine discovery. Hadst thou told me plainly, in any single text, that the Father, Son, and Holy Spirit are three real distinct persons in thy Divine nature, I had never suffered myself to be bewildered in so many doubts, nor embarrassed with so many strong fears of assenting to the mere inventions of men, instead of Divine doctrine; but I should have humbly and immediately accepted thy words, so far as it was possible for me to understand them, as the only rule of my faith. Or hadst thou been pleased so to express and include this proposition in the several scattered parts of thy book, from whence my reason and conscience might with ease find out and with certainty infer this doctrine, I should have joyfully employed all my reasoning powers, with their utmost skill and activity, to have found out this inference, and ingrafted it into my soul."

"Thou hast taught me, Holy Father, by thy prophets, that the way of holiness in the times of the Gospel, or under the kingdom of the Messiah, shall be a highway, a plain and easy path; so that the wayfaring man, or the stranger, 'though a fool, shall not err therein.' And thou hast called the poor and the ignorant, the mean and the foolish things of this world, to the knowledge of thyself and thy Son, and taught them to receive and partake of the salvation which thou hast provided. But how can such weak creatures ever take in so strange, so difficult, and so abstruse a doctrine as this, in the explication and defence whereof multitudes of men, even men of learning and piety, have lost themselves in infinite subtilties of dispute, and endless mazes of darkness? And can this strange and perplexing notion of three real persons going to make up one true God be so necessary and so important a part of that Christian doctrine, which, in the Old Testament and the New, is represented as so plain and so easy, even to the meanest understandings?"

Such were the last thoughts of a pious and learned man, after more than twenty years of examination of the Scriptures. They are full of instruction to us, and well calculated to confirm us in our present belief. If such a man as Dr. Watts was *forced out* of Trinitarianism by prayerful and conscientious study of the Bible, we, as Unitarians, have reason to thank God and take courage.

THE ATONEMENT.

FOR IF, WHEN WE WERE ENEMIES, WE WERE RECONCILED TO GOD BY THE DEATH OF HIS SON, MUCH MORE, BEING RECONCILED, WE SHALL BE SAVED BY HIS LIFE; AND NOT ONLY SO, BUT WE ALSO JOY IN GOD THROUGH OUR LORD JESUS CHRIST, BY WHOM WE HAVE NOW RECEIVED THE ATONEMENT. — Romans v. 10, 11.

THE word which is translated *reconcile* in the tenth verse, is translated *atone* in the eleventh. Of course, therefore, the meaning is the same. The two words were used by the translators as exactly synonymous, and the word Atonement was printed in the first editions of the English Bible, At-one-ment. It is used in the same manner by other writers in the time of James I., so that its meaning is well established, and as this is the only passage in the New Testament where it occurs, we are authorized to say that the doctrine of Atonement and the doctrine of Reconciliation are the same thing. If we so regard it, this is the great doctrine of religion. It is the substance of religion itself. Other truths may be important, but they are so only as they are subsidiary to this. In a practical point of view, they concern us only as they teach us how to be reconciled to God, and help us in becoming so. Or, in other words, all religious truth is important in proportion as it shows to sinners the way of salvation, and helps them to walk therein until salvation is attained.

The necessity of reconciliation rests upon the fact that we are sinners. "God made man upright, and he has sought out many inventions." "For there is not a just man upon earth, that doeth good, and sinneth not." How this came to pass is not here the material question. The fact is undeniable, and from it comes the necessity of the Gospel redemption. If there is any man who has committed no sin, for him the mission of Christ has no personal interest. "God was in Christ reconciling the world to himself," but where there has been no rebellion, there can be no reconciliation. "They that are whole need not a physician, but they that are sick"; and therefore Christ said, that "he came not to call the righteous, but sinners, to repentance." It is because we feel ourselves to be sinners, that we come to Christ. We have lost our way and desire to find it. We have rebelled against God and desire to make peace with him. We are alienated from him and desire to be again brought near. Our sins rise up in judgment against us, and we desire that the record of them should be blotted out. Through sin we are at enmity with God, and as his creatures, dependent on his power, as his children, whose only hope of happiness comes from the Father's love, our chief concern, I may say our only concern, is to find the means of reconciliation with him; to obtain assurance of pardon and acceptance with God, of whose love we have made ourselves so unworthy.

This is our inquiry to-night. Not an abstract subject of metaphysical research, but the great practical question of religion. How shall the burdened conscience throw off its load? Where shall the despairing heart, self-accused find hope? Where shall the weary and heavy laden find rest? Is it not a question which concerns us all? May God in his mercy guide us to a right answer! And that we may be so guided, let us consider it, not as a disputed subject in theology, but as a practical subject in vital religion.

How shall the sinner be reconciled with God? How shall he be *justified*, or restored to God's favor? How shall he obtain forgiveness and remission of sins? We look for an answer, — First, to the laws of God's government; to that which we call Nature, interpreted by our unenlightened reason. An answer comes, but it is not an answer of peace. It is not forgiveness, but "Pay me that thou owest." "If thou doest well, shalt thou not be accepted? and if thou doest not well, *sin lieth at the door.*" It is the voice of stern, unpitying exaction. " Everywhere in Nature we read Law, inexorable, unrelenting Law. She governs by laws, which indeed are always adapted to the good of the whole, to the advancement and perfection of the race, but beneath them the individual continually is crushed. Nature never pardons. Her wheels thunder along their iron track, nor turn out to spare any helpless mortal who has fallen beneath them. Ignorance of the law is no excuse. Helplessness is no exemption. There is no appeal to any court of error, but prompt execution follows judgment. The innocent child, who ignorantly touches fire, is not the less burned. The man who, in the night, ignorantly walks over a precipice, is not tho less destroyed. In nature, therefore, we find no word of pardon for those who have broken the law, whatever may be their excuse or sorrow."* If the laws of God's moral government are equally stern and unbending, there is no

---

* Doctrine of Forgiveness, by James F. Clarke.

hope for man; his sins will surely find him out, and sooner or later will work his destruction.

If we look to our own moral nature, the same answer comes, equally stern, equally unpitying. Perhaps I may say even more so. The wound upon the physical frame will be healed by the curative power of nature herself, and although a scar is left, the injury may be forgotten. But the wounds of conscience are not healed; sin once committed can never be forgotten. Or if for a time it be put out of mind by the hurried pursuits of life, it will still rise up again, like the ghost of a murdered friend, to spoil our best enjoyment and to rebuke us in our proudest imaginings. Conscience speaks no word of pardon; it gives no assurance that God's favor will be restored to those by whom it has been once forfeited. Its rebuke is equally stern for a sin committed years ago as for those of yesterday. The intervening years may have been spent in the sorrow of repentance, or in works of obedience, but conscience remains unappeased. Perhaps the more nearly we come to a righteous life, the more deeply we feel the stings of remorse, for the iniquity of bygone days.

Such is the natural working of a tender conscience. It cannot find comfort for itself; it cannot blot out the record of its own sins. It looks upward, but it clothes the Almighty in attributes of vengeance; its own fears read anger in his face; its own sense of ill-deserving anticipates the sentence of condemnation. It drives the sinner to cruel penances, to self-torture and scourging, vainly striving to expiate the sins of the soul by the sufferings of the body; and yet, after years of such penance, the poor sufferer, at each renewed remembrance of his sin, will strike the bleeding scourge more deeply into the flesh and cast himself to the ground in renewed and hopeless agony. History will tell of a thousand such, and this is the Voice of Pardon which the awakened conscience speaks.

Or sometimes it will deceive the sinner with the hope, that by offering payment to the Most High his debts may be discharged; and thus, by sacrifices upon the altar, or by the building of costly churches, or by the splendor of external worship, or, in more enlightened times, by institutions of charity and other works of philanthropy, men have sought to make their peace with Him against whose majesty they have rebelled. But still, however costly the sacrifice, the conscience cannot be thus satisfied. Still there has been a whispering, that it is not possible for the blood of bulls and goats to take away sin; or that God should be appeased by the imperfect offerings of those who, when they have done all, are but unprofitable servants.

There needed something more than this, some higher and better teaching. It is a necessity which every one of us, who acknowledges himself to be a sinner, must feel, and we shall feel it more and more deeply, in proportion as we rise higher in purity and goodness. We need to be assured that God is merciful. Reason itself may teach us that he is good towards those who do not violate his laws; for the provisions of nature are always bountiful and kind, both for man and beast, so long as they are not perverted by the selfishness or folly of those for whose good they were intended. But from the retributions of a violated law, reason alone finds no way of escape. From the anger of an offended God, reason alone points out no refuge. There is a debt which cannot be paid, and reason alone gives no assurance that God will remit it. This is wha we need to learn, *that God is merciful.* This is the balm in Gilead, by which the wounded conscience can be made whole; this is the voice from heaven which we need to hear, speaking peace to the broken and contrite heart. We need some assurance, that, "if we confess our sins, God is faithful and just to forgive our sins and to cleanse us from all unrighteousness."

The religion which can give us that assurance is the religion for which the sinful heart yearns. Let us but learn that there is forgiveness with God, that upon certain conditions, with which we are able to comply, he will not impute to men their past offences, but will *freely justify* them and graciously accept them, in the exercise of his infinite mercy, and it is all we need to know. The wall of separation between us and our God is then thrown down. The way for reconciliation, and for the redemption which follows it, is open. He who brings that assurance, who instructs us in these conditions, is indeed our Saviour. But if he not only does this, but gives us encouragement and help in complying with the conditions, and goes before in the way wherein we must walk, and disarms death of its terror, and reveals God to us as a Father clothed in the attributes of tenderness and love, and opens to our eyes the heavenly abode where God and his angels dwell, and to which he, the messenger of love, has gone before to prepare a place for us, that where he is we may be also;—in what words can we express our gratitude, except to say, "Thanks be to God, for his unspeakable gift," in our Lord Jesus Christ.

Such are the glad tidings of great joy, "Glory to God in the highest, and on earth peace, good-will toward men." Whisperings of the same message had been spoken in the world before. To Abraham and to his children, to the righteous men and prophets of olden time, some intimations had been given of God's abounding love towards the sinner: "For I have no pleasure, saith the Lord God, in the death of the sinner, but rather that he should turn and live."

By such words many hearts had been comforted. The penitent sinner had been made to hear joy and gladness, and the bones which had been broken were made to rejoice. Nay, I believe that in all religions, even in those most obscured by superstition, there have always been some rays of divine truth, received through the first revelation which God made of himself to his human family, by which a stronger hope of God's mercy has been given than reason alone could suggest. The spirit of God has always striven with man; the light has always been in the world everywhere, and men have preferred darkness rather than light because their deeds were evil. But when, through the manifold corruptions of sin and human error, the whole head had become sick and the whole heart faint, it became necessary that a clearer revelation of God's mercy should be made. And it was then, when the full time had come, that " God sent his Son into the world, not to condemn the world, but that the world through him might be saved."

The Christian religion is throughout a revelation of mercy; even as we read, " Of his fulness have we all received, and grace for grace." I do not mean that it annuls God's law; on the contrary, Christ came to fulfil, or to make perfect and complete, the moral law under which we live and by which we must be judged. The Christian law of morals is the strictest that has ever been given to man. It is the strictest that we can conceive. It takes hold, not only of the actions, but the motives from which action springs; of all our secret desires and thoughts and purposes. It holds before us the standard of absolute perfection, of which it gives an example in Jesus Christ, and commands us never to be weary of well-doing, until we have attained to the fulness of his stature. But for the past offences of the penitent sinner, and for his continued short-comings in the Christian race, it has words of blessed healing, of heavenly comfort, of eternal encouragement. "If any man sin, we have an advocate with the Father, even Jesus Christ the righteous."

When we have learned with humility of heart to confess our sins, to acknowledge ourselves guilty before God, and that by the deeds of the law — by our own imperfect righteousness — no man can be justified in his sight, then do we also learn, that God is ready to *justify us*, to restore us again to his favor, if we come before him with believing, trustful hearts, seeking to do his will as followers of Christ. That he will justify us; not because we deserve it, for from such a claim every mouth is stopped, by the acknowledgment of sin. But that he will justify us freely, by his grace, his infinite mercy, through the redemption that is in Christ Jesus, whom he hath foreordained to be a mercy-seat for those who approach through faith in him, to declare that the sinner shall be justified — treated as though he were righteous, received to the arms of God's love, even as the returning prodigal was received by his father — by the remission of sins that are past, through the forbearance of God. This was Christ's mission; to declare God's justification of the repenting sinner. That he might show God to be at the same time just and the justifier of him who believeth in Jesus.

We can therefore rely upon the mercy of God; we can feel sure that, if we go to him as children to a father, he will receive us; "he will in no wise cast us out." But we cannot claim the merit of this reception; it is not because of what *we* have done, and all the boasting of the self-righteous is excluded. It is to God's mercy alone, in Jesus Christ, that we owe our acceptance. The prime and perhaps only condition on which we receive forgiveness of our past sins is an act which, by its nature, excludes merit. It is an act of self-renunciation; the prostration before God of the self-convicted sinner; the act of sincere confession and repentance; in a word, the act of self-surrender to God, which by the Scripture is called Faith. Not belief only, that belief which the devils also may have even while they tremble; not that belief which is often an exercise of the barren intellect, and is no more than the willing or unwilling acceptance of certain opinions; but Faith, which is the deepest experience of the soul, — an act by which our whole relation towards God is changed; by which we are brought from the attitude of distrust and rebellion to that of children who, although with tears in their eyes, exclaim, Abba, my Father! — this is Christian faith.

This is the condition on which God has promised, through Christ, to forgive our sins. If it be fulfilled, he has promised that the record of the past shall be blotted out. At the foot of the cross, where we learn to believe, the burden falls from our back, and we start forward upon a new race with heaven in our view. A long and arduous race, — but we begin it with light hearts, full of hope, sure of obtaining the prize, if we run with patience, looking unto Jesus who is the author and finisher of our faith.

The law of God is therefore not made void. We acknowledge its full force by that act of faith, which is the condition of pardon. We place ourselves under the condemnation of God's law; we wait for sentence to be passed upon us; and instead thereof, hear the words of the Divine Saviour, "Depart in peace, thy faith hath saved thee"; "Go and sin no more."

The law of God is not made void; it is established as completely as if its utmost penalty had been exacted. The continuance of God's favor is also made to depend upon a renewed life, a life of filial obedience, without which we again fall into condemnation.

Nay, something more than this is true. The forgiveness of sin does not remove all evil consequences. It removes the worst, which is our estrangement from God, but there are others which remain. Although we may be restored to his favor and may feel in our hearts the earnest of heavenly bliss, it requires long years of striving to rid our souls of the stains which sin has left there.

The intemperate man may be reformed, he may feel that his reconciliation with God is made, but will the evil effects of past transgression quickly disappear? Will not even the appetite for that which was his ruin remain and return upon him, a morbid craving for that which he strives to hate? And so it is with all our sins. We may repent of them, we may forsake them, we may feel that through God's mercy in Jesus Christ they are forgiven, and yet their evil consequences may remain,— increasing the difficulty of our onward progress, returning upon us in perverted tastes, in sinful imaginings, in weakness of resolution, so that we are often compelled to exclaim, " That which we do, we allow not, but that which we would not, we do." Such is the true experience of the sinner, even of him who has found hope in Christ. It is a further vindication of God's law; it is a further evidence that those who trifle with their souls incur a dreadful risk, and must, to a certain extent, reap that which they sow.

God may forgive them, but he still leaves a token in their souls, by which they may see how narrow has been their escape. They may be saved, but it is so as by fire. Therefore it is that the redeemed in Christ, while they labor to work out their own salvation, must do it with fear and trembling. Thus, again, do we see that the law of God is not made void by the terms of reconciliation which he offers, yea, it is rather established.

One part, therefore, of the doctrine of reconciliation we can understand perfectly. I mean, so far as it requires a change in us. The change from worldliness to devotion; from rebellion to childlike self-surrender; from distrust to faith; from self-seeking and pride to self-denial and humility. It is a change which begins in a renewed heart and is completed in a renewed life. This is our reconciliation to God. We also understand how it is effected in us. By the knowledge of the truth as it is in Jesus; by the messages of love which he brings to us from the Father; by his holy example; by his instructions in righteousness; by his sufferings and death; by his promises of eternal life; by his resurrection from the dead; by his ascension into heaven; by his intercession for us with the Father; and by the influences of the Holy Spirit, which are given through him; — by the whole Gospel dispensation.

It is not only that Christ has taught us of the Father, but much more, because the Father is manifest in the Son. The Divine attributes, however explained to us, we could but imperfectly understand. We might still have a lingering fear, that the justice of an Infinite Being could not be satisfied, without the full punishment of the offender. But when we read the history of Christ himself, the image of the invisible God, and see how perfectly justice and mercy are joined together in him, not as conflicting attributes, but as only different exhibitions of the same parental love, stern or gentle, according to the necessity of each case, we can understand how God is just and the justifier of those who believe in Jesus; how he can condemn sin and yet pardon the sinner; "not desiring the death of any, but that all should turn to him and live." It is thus that Christ showed himself to us, and it is in this attribute of justice, tempered by mercy, that we receive him as the manifestation of the

Father, — the Word made flesh. We contend that there is no view of God's justice, which can be correct, that does not find its manifestation and development in Christ.

Such is the effect on us, and such are the means by which it is produced. This is therefore the practical part of our subject. So far as we are concerned in the work of reconciliation with God, this is all that we need to know. We know that God is willing to receive us; we know the conditions on which we shall be received; every motive for coming to him, and every encouragement, is given; we see from what source help will come to our infirmities; we know enough of God's counsels to be sure that our seeking will not be in vain.

Upon all this there is scarcely any controversy among Christians. Here, as in almost all other doctrines, the controversy is not concerning that which is practical, for the practical is almost always plain. It concerns questions to which we can give no positive answer. It is upon subjects which are for the great part beyond our reach. There are some points of difficulty of this sort in the doctrine of atonement; questions of theology, rather than of religion. Such for example as these: In the work of reconciliation, is not a change in God also needed, as well as in us? How did the death of Christ make it safe for God to forgive sin in a sense in which it was not before safe? What effect upon the counsels of God does the mediation of Christ produce? In what sense did Christ die for us and suffer in our stead? The questions are of great interest, but while I state them you see that they are chiefly above our comprehension. We may speculate concerning them, but cannot arrive at certain conclusions. We shall attempt to answer them, however, so far as the Scripture guides us next Sunday evening.

THE ATONEMENT.

GOD WAS IN CHRIST, RECONCILING THE WORLD UNTO HIMSELF, NOT IMPUTING THEIR TRESPASSES UNTO THEM. — 2 Cor. v. 19.

In our inquiries last Sunday, we examined the more practical part of the doctrine of atonement or reconciliation. We saw that, to effect reconciliation with God, a radical change is needed in us. The question now arises, Is a corresponding change needed in God himself? Let me again say, that until we can penetrate more deeply into the Divine nature than we now can, it is a question to which we can give no clear answer.

Of all the attributes of God there is none more completely beyond our comprehension than his unchangeableness or immutability. We are taught, on the one hand, that in him there is no change, neither shadow of turning; but on the other, that he is a Father who pities his children, who does not afflict willingly, who answers our prayers, who forgives our sins. All of which implies that his countenance towards us changes, that his dealings with us change, that he regards us with different feelings at different times, according to the relation in which we stand towards him. I think that this is the general representation of God in the

Scriptures. He is shown to us, not as an abstract order of the universe, stern and unvarying, uninfluenced by prayer, unchanged by repentance, but as a Heavenly Father, with all the attributes of tenderness and compassion which belong to that name.

If that is the true representation, it seems impossible that his feelings should be the same towards the hardened rebel, and the repentant sinner, and the glorified saint. Our own hearts tell us that it cannot be. Yet if God is immutable, how can it be otherwise? Some will answer, that he is like the sun in the heavens, always shining with clear and benignant rays; and that the clouds which veil him from our eyes, namely our sins, work no change in him, although they change his relation toward us. Perhaps it is a right answer, but I confess it seems to me to make our whole relations with God too mechanical. The heart yearns for personal affection. We long for the smile of approbation, not a seeming smile, but the real smile of tenderness and parental love. Whether it is weakness or not, I do not know, but I am sure that our hearts are more moved by the representation of God in the parable of the Prodigal Son, where the Father cannot wait to be sought for, but goes out to meet his returning child and falls upon his neck and kisses him, than by all the abstract arguments of God's unchanging goodness that have ever been written. It may be unphilosophical, but perhaps, when we know more, we shall find that the philosophy which requires us to be untrue to our nature is "falsely so called."

I cannot but look with suspicion upon any system of religion which philosophizes away our natural affections. When we lie under the burden of sin, our hearts tell us that we are at enmity with God, and that he is thereby estranged from us. Not that he regards us with any thing like human anger, for he loves us even then; but there is the estrangement which holiness must feel towards sin. There is a desire for our return and the feeling of approbation, the renewal of that kind of love which had been withdrawn, when we come to him and say, "Father, we have sinned against Heaven and before thee." In our theory, we may say that there is no change; but it is a theory which our feelings do not recognize. It is an intuition of our nature that God loves us in a different sense, when we return to him, from that in which he loved us before.

You will see, however, from my whole manner of speaking, that I do not believe in such a change in God as is sometimes taught. Many persons teach the doctrine of atonement as though the chief difficulty were on the side of God, and not on that of the sinner. They speak of God's being reconciled to man, much more than of man's being reconciled to God. They represent God as having been full of anger, of vindictive wrath, ready to hurl punishment upon sinners, unwilling and unable to forgive them, until his anger was appeased by the sufferings and death of Christ, who endured the punishment of the guilty.

We reject this view, first, because the Scripture uniformly represents that the cause of Christ's coming into the world was not the wrath of God, but his love. "God so loved the world, that he gave his only-begotten Son, that whosoever believeth in him should have everlasting life." "Herein is love, not that we loved God, but that God loved us, and sent his Son to be the propitiation for our sins." And still more strongly, "In this was manifested the love of God towards us, because that God sent his only-begotten Son into the world, that we might live through him." I repeat, that this is not the occasional, but the uniform, statement of the Scripture. There is no passage which says or implies that God's anger with the sinner was the cause of Christ coming, or that Christ came to make him merciful. His coming was a proof of mercy; it was the *effect* of God's love. God's anger is not of a kind that needs to be appeased.

Another reason why we reject such a theory of God's anger is this: The Scriptures represent that Christ is the manifestation of God. In his character, therefore, we learn the attributes of God. This is our best instruction concerning the meaning of God's justice and mercy, of his anger and love. But according to the view of the Divine wrath just now considered, God and Christ are placed in the strongest contrast; one all anger, the other all love; one all justice, the other all mercy; one seeking to punish, the other seeking to save. Such a view cannot be correct. God is love, and Christ is the image of his love. In no respect is the Son more perfectly the manifestation of the Father than in this.

Thirdly: We are confirmed in this view, because there is not a single passage in the Bible in which God is said to be reconciled to man, but always that man is to be reconciled to God. "For if, when we were enemies, we were reconciled to God by the death of his Son, much more, being reconciled, we shall be saved by his life." Rom. v. 10. "All things are of God, who hath reconciled us to himself by Jesus Christ, and hath given to us the ministry of reconciliation; namely, that God was in Christ reconciling the world unto himself, not imputing their trespasses unto them, and hath committed unto us the word of reconciliation. Now then we are ambassadors for Christ, as though God did beseech you by us, Be ye reconciled to God." 2 Cor. v. 18 – 20. Here is a full statement of the subject before us. It is God pleading with us through Christ, as a Father pleads with his erring children. He is ready to be reconciled to them, whenever they will come to him. He encourages them to come, he waits for them, he goes out to meet them. In the work of reconciliation which must be effected before they can be received, the *difficulty* is not on his part, but on theirs alone.

If, therefore, we admit that a change takes place in the feelings of God towards the returning sinner, it is not a change from vindictive wrath to overflowing love, from a God who is all justice to a God of all mercy, but it is a change from one kind of love to another. As the earthly parent loves his children, both when they are rebellious and when they are repentant, so does God love us all and always. If it is a different kind of love, it arises from the necessity of the case, in the dealings of a being infinitely holy towards those who are frail and sinful.

We think that no other view of God is either Scriptural or reasonable. It presents him to us, not only as a God, but as a Father, wise in his compassion; in whom the attributes of justice and mercy are only the different exercise of the same love.

The next question which arises is this: What effect upon the counsels of God does the mediation of Christ produce? By the mediation of Christ we mean, not only his sufferings and death, but the whole Gospel dispensation. His coming down from heaven, his instructions, his life and holy example, his precepts, his sufferings and death, his resurrection, his ascension into heaven at the right hand of the Father, to make intercession for us. This is the whole Gospel dispensation. We understand it all to be included in Christ's work as the mediator between God and man.

What effect did it produce upon the counsels of God towards the sinner? Here again our limited faculties present a difficulty. It is a question which we cannot answer perfectly, until by our searching we can find out God, and enter into the secret places of his wisdom. We believe the Gospel dispensation was *needful*. It does not express the whole truth to say that the coming of Christ was desirable, as a means of salvation, for it was indispensable. From the beginning, it was a part of God's counsel towards man. It is an essential link in the chain, by which God draws the sinner to himself. In the plan of salvation we cannot dispense with Christ: "No man," he says, "can come to the Father but by me." "I am the vine, ye are the branches. As the branch cannot bear fruit of itself, except it abide in the vine, no more can ye, except ye abide in me." Words cannot express more strongly than these, the personal necessity of Christ to us. I could give you a hundred instances of the same sort, teaching in the strongest terms our dependence upon the Gospel dispensation, for the hope, and in the work, of salvation.

But if you ask me why God has so appointed, or if he could not have devised some other means by which the same gracious work would have been accomplished, you ask me unwisely, and it would be unwise in me to attempt an answer. It is enough for us that there is one way; that if we come to God in penitence and faith, as Christ has taught us to come, we shall find forgiveness and acceptance with him; that under the Gospel dispensation there is no stumbling-block in our path to heaven, except deliberate and continued sin. If we are delivered from the body of this death, we should thank God, through our Lord Jesus Christ, without being too curious to know whether God could not have found some other means, equally effectual, for our deliverance.

There is no difficulty in the belief that man's salvation

depends upon the mediation of Christ. Consider it either as a work done for us, or as a prayer offered for our sake. In either case, the Scripture doctrine of the absolute necessity of Christ's coming, and of his sufferings and death, is according to the analogy of God's general dealing with us and to our belief as Christians in the efficacy of prayer. Nearly all the blessings which come to the world, come through the faithful exertions of the good. It is to the holy throng of apostles and martyrs, God's saints on earth, that all progress in wisdom and goodness, and all triumphs over evil, are due. If they had not lived, or if they had been unfaithful, a thousand blessings for which we are now thankful would never have reached us. It is in accordance with the same law, although in a higher exemplification of it, that the work of Christ was performed. We may not understand its full efficacy, but we can understand its necessity, and that from its faithful performance our salvation proceeds.

And so, if we consider Christ's mediation as a prayer, or continued intercession with God for our sake, the Scriptural doctrine of its efficacy presents no greater difficulty than the doctrine of prayer in general. We believe that our prayers are answered; that God is more ready to give his Holy Spirit to those that ask him, than an earthly parent is to bestow good gifts upon his children. But who shall explain this? Who shall tell us how prayer is answered? How can human asking change the mind of God towards us? We do not know, yet our affections, our inward experience, not less than the Scriptures, assure us that prayer is answered; that by prayer, and in answer to prayer, we obtain blessings which otherwise would never come to us. Nor can I perceive any greater unreasonableness in the belief that our prayers, one for another, are answered

It is an instinct to pray for those we love. We cannot explain how the prayer can bring the blessing, but yet we cannot help praying. Such spiritual instincts should not be slighted because they are beyond the reach of intellect. To me they carry their own evidence. I believe in GOD, not so much because it can be proved by argument, as because it is a necessity of my nature. For the same reason I believe in prayer, and the Scripture strongly confirms the belief. It teaches that the effectual, fervent prayer of a righteous man availeth much. If we knew more of God, and of the spiritual world, and of the laws by which all spiritual beings are bound together in one mysterious chain, from the lowest to the highest, we might be able to understand how the prayers of the good may be answered in behalf of the wicked, and that the nearer to God we come in purity and love, the more effectual our prayers will be. We then might understand how the intercession of one like Jesus, the beloved Son of God, can be an indispensable influence and a real agency in the redemption of the world. Such, at least, is the Scriptural doctrine, and as such we are content to receive it. Christ then becomes to us the living head of the Church. He is not only our benefactor through his life and sufferings on earth, but he also liveth to make intercession for us with the Father. In our strugglings against sin and our efforts to rise, it is an unspeakable comfort to know, that we have the sympathy and prayers and spiritual aid of one so pure and good, who was tempted in all points as we are, yet without sin, who was made perfect through suffering, and is now exalted at the right hand of God.

We now proceed to a point which has involved much discussion and given rise to a multitude of theories. How **did** the sufferings and death of Christ make it *safe* for God to forgive sin, in a sense in which it was not before safe? There are some who say, that it was by Christ's suffering the full penalty of sin, and thereby making full satisfaction to the law, that he enabled the sinner to go free. A theory which we cannot receive, chiefly for two reasons.

First, it leaves no room for God's mercy. If a debt is fully paid, we owe thanks to him who paid it, but not to him who exacts the payment. Such is not the doctrine of the Bible, which teaches us that God freely forgives; that our trespasses are not imputed to us, " through his forbearance," not through his exaction of the penalty from another. Christ teaches us to pray, " Forgive us our trespasses, as we forgive those who trespass against us," which is not consistent with the idea of the debts being paid, either by the offender himself, or by any one else for him. If a debt is paid, there can be a release, but, properly speaking, there is no room for remission.

Secondly, the chief penalty of sin, the only real penalty, is remorse of conscience and estrangement from God, and by the nature of the soul no one can endure this penalty for another. As a matter of fact, also, Christ did not endure it. No remorse of conscience ever visited him. However mysterious and inexplicable his sufferings may have been, this never made any part of them. Never for a moment did he feel estrangement from God; never for a moment was the love of God withdrawn from him. In the agony of human suffering, he exclaimed, " My God, my God, why hast thou forsaken me?" But perhaps even these words were spoken, as calling to his mind the whole of the triumphant psalm of David from which they are taken; and even in that dreadful hour we perceive his nearness to God, in the comforting words spoken to the repentant criminal, and in his prayer for his enemies, and in his dying words, " Into thy hands I commend my spirit.' No ; Christ truly suffered, the just for the unjust, but he did not suffer as a sinner, and therefore he did not suffer the punishment of sin. By the blindness of human judgment, he was numbered among the transgressors, and suffered an ignominious and cruel death, but he was always the beloved Son, in whom God was well pleased. He was never nearer to God, he was never further removed from the punishment of sin, than when his sufferings for our sake were the most terrible.

We cannot believe, therefore, in the theory of Christ's sufferings just stated. But we can perceive that in another way the Gospel dispensation, in which we include the sufferings and death of Christ, has made it safe that sin should be forgiven, under God's moral government, in a sense in which it might not otherwise have been safe. The two essential requisites to make pardon safe are these : first, to secure in the offender such a disposition as will lead him to a true and permanent reformation ; and secondly, to maintain the sanctity of the law so that it shall not be brought into contempt, but that, while the sinner is forgiven, his abhorrence of sin may be increased, and the heinousness of sin, in God's sight, be made more plainly to appear. When these two requisites are attained, forgiveness of sin becomes safe. It is safe to the sinner himself, because his reformation is secure ; it is safe to the moral government of God, because his law is not brought into contempt, but is honored even more highly. This is precisely the result which the Gospel dispensation accomplishes. It arouses the sinner to those emotions, by which alone his reconciliation with God can be effected, and his reformation secured,— the emotions of repentance, of self-renunciation, of love —which are in themselves a complete renewal of the inward life, and thus brings him to such a relation towards God, that the word of pardon can be safely spoken.

Such has been the experience of hundreds of thousands. The ministry of Christ, and especially his sufferings and death, have been the influence by which more souls have been aroused from the sleep of sin, than by all others beside. But at the same time the hatred of sin has been increased. The manner in which pardon is brought to the sinner is the most dreadful condemnation of sin. It is offered to us at the expense of so much suffering, that when we read the account of it, we lament our sins, by which it was made necessary, more bitterly than at any other time. If it had been proclaimed from heaven, that God is ready to forgive the repenting sinner, the message would have been the same that we have now received, but how different would have been the effect! We might then indeed have supposed that sin is a light evil, and its record easily blotted out. But when we read the narrative of Christ's sufferings, we perceive how heinous sin must be in the sight of God our consciences are awakened to discern how terrible it consequences must be, here and hereafter. If it were a small evil, if escape from it were easy, if its consequences were temporary and trivial, would the Heavenly Father have appointed his holy child Jesus to a life of such suffering, and to a death of such agony, for its removal? We think not; nay, we are sure that it could not be. The whole Gospel dispensation, as God has directed it, impresses us deeply with the awfulness of sin; it brings before us the vision of its terrible consequences more distinctly, by its accents of love mingled with the records of suffering, than could have been done by the most fearful threats of punishment, or the most vindictive execution of the law.

Something of the same benignant purpose we see in

God's general providence. It is through the suffering and sacrifices of the good, through their pains, self-denials and martyrdoms, that the sins of the wicked receive their sternest rebuke, and the sinner himself is reformed. Nor are there any circumstances, under which we hate our sins so much, as when suffering is endured by those whom we love, for the sake of their removal. How much more do we feel this, when brought home to us by the sufferings of one at the same time so pure and so exalted as Jesus Christ! In proportion as we believe in them, the effect is deepened; it grows with our spiritual growth, it strengthens with our spiritual strength. It is not a mysterious influence, but natural and unavoidable; the working of the human heart, when softened by the dews of God's grace. It leads to the perfect vindication of the sacredness of God's law, at the same time that pardon is offered to the sinner and his return to righteousness secured.

There is one other question under the doctrine of Atonement, which we must consider, although in but very few words. In what sense did Christ die *for us?* The language of Scripture with reference to it is various and strong, — sometimes figurative, sometimes literal, sometimes obscure. He is our ransom, our sacrifice, our sin-offering; he is made sin for us, he bore our punishment, the chastisement of our peace is laid upon him, by his stripes we are healed; he has borne our griefs, he was bruised for our iniquities, and the Lord hath laid upon him the iniquity of us all. All of this is Scriptural language. What does it mean? A part of it is manifestly figurative, as when it is said "he hath made him to be sin for us," and "upon him is laid the iniquity of us all." Some persons have understood even this literally, and thus Martin Luther taught that Christ was the greatest sinner, murderer, robber, and the like, that the world ever saw, because all the sins of all the world were accumulated in him, to receive their condemnation and their punishment. I do not know what men mean, when they use such language, and it is charitable to suppose that they do not know themselves. There is no danger of any one using it at the present day, and no need of proving its absurdity.

In the same manner the word *ransom* has been interpreted literally, and some of the Christian Fathers taught that the sufferings of Christ were the ransom, or purchase-money, paid by God and received by the enemy of souls, the Devil, as the price of the sinner's release. We shall not follow such interpretations further; they belong to days gone by, and are a monument of human weakness.

The whole language which we have quoted we think means no more nor less than this: that Christ suffered for us, the just for the unjust, to bring us to God. Whatever is expressed more than these words imply is figurative, and not literal. The sufferings and death of Christ were necessary as a means of our redemption from sin; they were therefore endured in consequence or on account of our sins; they were our ransom, the price paid for us, the cost of our deliverance. "The chastisement of our peace was laid upon him," because this was the means through which our peace was obtained. "By his stripes we are healed," because the healing of our souls, in the forgiveness of our sins, is the result of that dispensation of which his sufferings were a needful part. "We are washed in his blood," because the shedding of his blood leads to our cleansing. He suffered and died in our stead, (although this is not a Scriptural expression,) because *his* sufferings and death save *us* from condemnation. As to all this language, there has been much disputing about words. I find in orthodox creeds and books a great deal to which I cannot assent. But whenever I converse with individuals who receive such creeds, and learn what they mean by the words used, the differences gradually fade away. I believe that the majority of them hold in fact nearly the same doctrine which I have now explained. Even when they speak of a *vicarious* atonement, they very often mean no more than we can accept. There is a plain and real sense in which I can use that word, for it is true that Christ suffered *for us*, and by this means, through the grace of God, we escape the suffering which our sins would otherwise have brought upon us. If he had not come upon earth and fulfilled his ministry, we must have died in our sins, for we are not able to guide ourselves nor save ourselves, and it is through him alone that we come near to God. There may be others who believe more than these words convey, and who teach that the wrath of God was literally laid on Jesus Christ; but I seldom meet them, and think that their number is daily becoming less. For ourselves, we are satisfied to know that "God commendeth his love towards us, in that, while we were yet sinners, Christ died for us." The way for our return to God is open, and he is waiting to be gracious.

REGENERATION

JESUS ANSWERED AND SAID UNTO HIM, VERILY, VERILY, I SAY UNTO THEE, EXCEPT A MAN BE BORN AGAIN, HE CANNOT SEE THE KINGDOM OF GOD. THAT WHICH IS BORN OF THE FLESH IS FLESH, AND THAT WHICH IS BORN OF THE SPIRIT IS SPIRIT.— John iii. 3, 6.

OUR subject this evening is the Christian doctrine of Regeneration, or the new birth; the nature of the change implied in those words, the means and agency by which it is produced, and the evidences by which we may judge of its reality. It is a subject whose importance all Christians acknowledge, for whatever views we take of it, as theologians, we must admit that in practical religion every thing depends upon its application. To ask who is regenerate is to ask who is a Christian. To become regenerate is to become a Christian. We may dispute as to what the new birth is, but we cannot dispute the Saviour's words, that "unless a man be born again, he cannot see the kingdom of God." There are some persons who suppose that Unitarians deny this doctrine. But there could not be a greater mistake. It would be the same as denying that a man can become a Christian, or that there is any real difference between good men and bad, between those who serve God and those who serve him not. There are some explanations of the doctrine which we reject, because they are unsound and unscriptural, but we do not reject the doctrine itself.

For example, we do not believe in an instantaneous and miraculous change, by virtue of which he who is at one moment totally depraved can become in the next one of God's saints. But we do believe, that by the blessing of God a radical change may begin at any time, by which the *direction* of a man's life may be changed from that which 'eads downward to that which leads upward.

We do not believe that this change will always be accompanied, either with the panic of an agonized conscience, or the ecstasies of rejoicing, but that its inward experience will be different in different individuals, according to their various temperament and education, to the degrees of their guilt, and to the influences under which they have been placed. The outward evidences of the change will also differ in an equal degree. I have seen men at a camp-meeting under such strong excitement, that they have been tied, hand and foot, to prevent them from some bodily injury; others pass through an equally strong experience, to whom the kingdom of God comes without observation. We do not deny the reality of the change effected in either case. We must judge of them both, as we judge of the tree, by its fruit. We give our preference indeed to the latter, because observation leads us to distrust all violent excitements. There is danger that they will not last, and that the spiritual fever will be followed by a corresponding and perhaps fatal prostration. This is particularly true, where the excitemen' is produced by artificial means, by the sympathy of crowds and the appliances of fear. At such times men are carried beyond their own convictions, and are very liable to be deceived as to their real feelings. The resu t very often is that after a few days they see every thing in a different light, and sometimes the Scripture is fulfilled in them, that the last stage of such men is worse than the first. We have greater confidence in the change which comes through the quietness of thought. It may promise less at first, but will accomplish more in the end. It may be accompanied with less of the rapture of religious triumph, but it is more likely to bring us to that peace which passeth all understanding. For such reasons, we do not enter into what are called "revivals of religion," and the protracted meetings by which they are generally excited. Our observation of them has not been favorable to their permanent usefulness. It is not that we deny the change of heart which is needed in becoming a Christian, nor that we would limit the action of God's spirit in producing it. We may rightly pray to him, "Revive thy work in the midst of the years"; and in the progress of every religious society, as in the experience of every individual, there will be times of awakening, in which the lukewarm become zealous, and the cold-hearted and sinful are rebuked. Such seasons of refreshing, when they come from the use of the ordinary Gospel means, are always to be welcomed, and their result is always good. But when they are brought on almost forcibly, by the use of what we may call religious machinery, it is quite a different thing. They are artificial in their origin and unnatural in their result. Their good effect, which seems at first very great, is seldom permanent. I have known instances in which, out of a hundred converts, less than one tenth held fast to their profession for six months. In such cases the evil is greater than the good, and it is from the fear of such results that we prefer more quiet modes of proceeding.

Once more: we believe that every real change in the

character and in the heart must be begun, continued, and ended in God. It is he "who worketh in us both to will and to do, of his good pleasure." In the Christian course from the very first to the last, we are dependent upon him. As in the natural world, the seed is formed by his creative power, and germinates and grows up and is developed into a plant or tree, through the benign influences of nature, which are only another name for the Divine working, so it is in the human soul that the seed of righteousness is at first planted, and is developed by the sweet influences of God's grace. With this difference, however, which should be carefully remarked, that in the latter case the soul must acknowledge the working of God and feel itself sustained by his presence. In proportion as we feel our dependence on God, we become strong. If we rely upon ourselves alone, we become weak. We are never so much in danger of falling, as when we boast in our hearts that we stand firmly. It is thus that God teaches us, by the practical experience of life, that we depend on him, that we are not sufficient to ourselves.

But while we receive this as the Scriptural doctrine of God's grace, we do not the less insist upon the necessity of our own working. In one sense, we depend for the whole work of our salvation, from the first dawning thought of goodness to the last complete triumph of Christian faith, upon the awakening and saving influences of God's spirit; and we can therefore join in the prayer of the poet, —

> "Direct, suggest, control, this day,
> All we design or do or say."

And in that of the Psalmist David, "Create in me a clean heart, O God, and renew a right spirit within me;" for it is the prayer not only of weakness, but of faith, and to every sincere Christian it will surely be answered. But on the other hand we too must work; we have no right to expect miracles to be done for us. We have no right to expect that the spirit of God will come to us unsought. God helps those who try to help themselves. He will not save us in spite of ourselves. It is of those who are striving to work out their own salvation with fear and trembling, that the Scripture says, " God worketh in them both to will and to do." To those only who use what they already have is it promised that more will be given.

Nor can we separate the Divine working from that which we call the natural operation of our own minds, and the natural influences of our daily life. A thought of righteousness comes to the hardened sinner, he scarcely knows how, nor is it important that he should know. It is of God's sending, whether you call it the direct suggestion of his Spirit or not. It is an angel visitant, and if cordially received others will follow in its train, until the heart becomes the temple of the living God, full of his ministering spirits. From that first impulse towards goodness, as he advances, step by step, contending against sin, reaching towards heaven, the Christian can never tell exactly how much depends upon his own exertion, and how much upon a higher power. He knows that when his heart is full of prayer, he progresses most rapidly; but he also knows that a blessing never comes upon his indolence. He finds no encouragement to wait until God does his work, but no sooner does he take hold of it than he feels sure that God is helping him. He thus feels the equal necessity of his own exertions and of the Divine blessing, and is kept in that healthy progress of mind and character, which belongs to the true Christian life. Such we think is the wise ordering of God. In the influences of his Spirit upon the soul we cannot say, "Lo here! or Lo there!" "he cometh down like rain upon the mown grass, as showers that water the earth," and the proof of his coming is found in the fruits of righteousness, in pure and holy thoughts, in heavenly aspirings, and in every Christian grace.

It is supposed by many persons, that the doctrine of Regeneration depends upon what are called the doctrines of Original Sin and Total Depravity. This is a mistake which it is important to remove. We must therefore consider these doctrines for a few moments before going further. In fact, there are few persons who explain them at the present day in the same manner in which they were taught fifty years ago. The Calvinistic doctrine of original sin is, that in the fall of Adam the whole human race were made sinners; that in consequence thereof, sin is *imputed* to every human being at his birth, in such a sense that he is under the wrath of God and is subject to eternal damnation; that his nature, being essentially corrupt, is capable of no good thing, not even to wish or pray for good. Its best actions therefore are hateful in the sight of God, and absolute, total depravity is the necessary result of its development. For a nature such as this, there is but one hope of salvation, which is in the miraculous and irresistible grace of God. The change of heart is therefore, according to this view, an absolute change of nature, it comes not because of a man's own seeking, but irrespectively thereof. Those to whom it comes are thereby God's elect. Those to whom it does not come remain under the sentence of condemnation, from which they cannot by any means escape.

Such is the theory which Calvin taught. But I think very few of his adherents now receive it. It is so much modified, that, even when the same words are used, different ideas are conveyed. By original sin, the majority understand no more than original imperfection; and by the imputation of Adam's sin, no more than the evil consequences which the child inherits from his parents, in an impaired physical and mental constitution. In this sense, we believe in original sin. We are certainly born imperfect, with many tendencies to evil. These tendencies are also, to some extent, inherited. In this sense, the sins of the father may be said to be visited on the children, as I have known whole families to be born with depraved appetites, which have followed them to their graves. But if, on the one side, there are evil tendencies, there are, on the other, equally strong tendencies to good; amiable dispositions and a natural love of truth and purity. These also come to us in part as our birthright. We do not call them virtue or religion, nor do we say that these alone make us acceptable to God. Nor, on the other hand, do we say that the evil tendencies with which we are born make us hateful to God. In both cases, the natural constitution of our minds, together with all the circumstances of our birth and education, will be taken into account by a just and merciful God, in his final judgment of us. To whom much is given, of him much will be required. To whom little is given, of him little will be required. No one will be condemned because of the sins which his father committed, although he may suffer in consequence of them. "The soul that sinneth, it shall die." Such is the theory of original imperfection, which is sometimes improperly called original sin.

With regard also to total depravity, most persons who profess to believe it mean nothing more than this, that the best actions of a selfish and worldly man partake of his selfishness and worldliness; that until we have learned to deny ourselves and to take the law of God as our supreme law, our most amiable qualities partake of the character of sin In such a sense, therefore, you may say that the unregenerate man is totally depraved, because there is no part of his conduct or his character which is fully conformed to the Divine law. The pervading principle of his life is wrong, and, in this sense, all is wrong. Change that pervading principle, and you change every thing. It is like infusing healthy blood into the physical frame. It will gradually, but certainly, change every part of the physical and mental constitution.

We shall not follow this train of thought further. What I have said will serve my purpose to show, that, while the doctrines in question continue the same in words, they may be very different in idea.

The truth concerning our nature by birth, and the spiritual condition to which we are brought by regeneration, or the new birth, seems to be this. We are born with a mixed constitution, physical, intellectual, and moral. These, as they originally came from the creative hand of God, were pronounced to be good. The moral nature is the highest, that is the soul, and to this the physical and intellectual, the body and the mind, should minister. But, by the necessity of the case, the physical is developed first, " the first man is of the earth, earthy." Our first wants, our first enjoyments and sufferings, are purely physical. The first exercise of the faculty of thought takes that direction. Self-love, which is needful for self-preservation, is thus early developed. Self-indulgence in what is pleasant, and angry resistance to what is unpleasant, are the natural consequences. All this is not sinful, it is simply of the earth, earthy. It is our physical nature. Gradually the higher nature begins to appear. The sweet affections of the child, pure and truthful, begin to expand. A sense of right, of justice, and of truth, gradually shows itself. At first very weak, but also very correct, for the instincts of childhood upon all moral subjects are sure to be right. In the progress of development, the intellect adds strength either to the physical or moral constitution, according to the natural temperament and the circumstances of education and example.

The period when moral responsibility begins is hard to determine. It certainly does not begin until there is a clear perception of right and wrong, and a choice of one or the other; but whenever it begins, the child is conscious of difficulties. His first exercise, as a moral being, is a struggle, a conflict. There is an enemy to be conquered, a victory to be won. Conscience claims the supremacy; it says, Thou must, or Thou must not; but the body, with its wants and its enjoyments, resists its commands. Reason pleads for the right, passion and appetite for the wrong. It is the struggle of life commenced, the spirit against the flesh, and the flesh against the spirit. The result, if human weakness receives no heavenly aid, is but too evident. The physical, that is to say the powers of the flesh, being first developed, is strong and vigorous, while the moral has but an infant's strength and soon gives way. The passions gain strength by what they feed on; the intellect is brutalized and brought into their service; the conscience is buried under the accumulated rubbish of sin.

Even in Christian lands, and under the influences of Christian education and Christian example, which is a strong divine helping to the principle of right, the great majority of men and women, when they come to the age of mature life, find that the work of moral discipline is still to be accomplished. There is a difference in their degrees of sinfulness; but with nine ou of ten, the pervading principle of conduct is self-love, or self-indulgence, or worldly ambition. In nine cases out of ten, therefore, a radical change is needed, before they can properly be called Christians. I call it a radical change, for if you change the principle of life, as I have already said, you change every thing. It is not only an outward change, for the proprieties of life may already be observed. It is chiefly an inward change, which concerns the motives and the affections. In many instances where the outward conduct continues the same, the real change of character is equally great.

I have said, in nine cases out of ten, that such will be the result; perhaps I might have used even stronger language, for there are very few persons who are not under the necessity, sooner or later, of that strong moral exercise, through which, by the blessing of God, the worldly and selfish heart becomes religious. Sometimes it is a violent and short struggle, sometimes a slow and laborious self-discipline; sometimes we can tell the day and the hour when it begins, and sometimes we almost doubt whether it has commenced or not, until it is accomplished. But with nearly all, in some way or other, the change must be accomplished from the earthly to the spiritual, from the worldly to the religious, from the selfish to the self-denying character, after we have come to the years of conscious self-direction.

In a few instances, equally rare and beautiful, the development of our nature is so healthy, that the soul, almost from the first, asserts its rightful supremacy. This is sometimes the result of pure Christian influences, the wise training of parents, the example of good and pious teachers, which may be called the human agency by which the Divine Spirit is working. Sometimes, even when surrounded by the worst influences of sin, in the dens of iniquity, or in the high places of worldliness, the child is seen to grow up with almost stainless purity, through some mysterious guiding of which it is not conscious, but which leads heavenward, as by an angel's hand. In such cases there seems never to be a struggle between the flesh and the spirit. The soul grows up to the heavenly life, almost as the seed grows up to its appointed beauty. Yet I believe that, even in such cases, if we could understand the full working of the soul, we should find here, as elsewhere, what is called the new birth, which is the passing from the earthly or natural state to the spiritual or heavenly. It may take place very early and very gradually, but I think that it is not the less real. The life of the spirit is not that to which we are first born, but the life of the flesh. The second man, and not the first, is the Lord from heaven. When Christ is formed in the soul, it is the redemption of the soul from the natural earthly influence. If it is effected before that influence has brought degradation, the thanksgiving to God may be greater, but it is not less a redemption.

Upon this subject, however, I would not dispute. Such instances are as rare as they are blessed. With by far the greater part of the human family, the experience is very different and far more painful. We find ourselves laden with sins, we scarcely know how. We are walking in a wrong direction, almost before we have thought whither the path leads. Our first serious thoughts of heaven are awakened, by our seeing that our faces are not turned heavenward. It is the restlessness of the soul under the bondage of sin, that arouses us to assert its true dignity. Through some human agency, or through the working of our own mind, God speaks to us, and if we hearken, the conflict begins, the result of which is properly called a deliverance and a victory.

From what has been now said, although in a desultory manner, you will understand my views upon this important topic, the doctrine of Regeneration. By this new birth, we mean a change from the carnal to the spiritual; that is, not an absolute change of nature, which would be the creation of a new soul, but the subjection of the lower principles of our nature, which are of the flesh, to the higher principles, which are of the spirit. It is a change, therefore, in the motives and the affections, that is a change of heart. It is a new direction given both to the inward and outward life, and the whole meaning of life is thereby changed. I do not mean any thing mystical or mysterious by this; in proportion as we become religious persons, we shall understand it.

Secondly: It is a change needed by all. Sooner or later it must be experienced by all, before they can be called the followers of Christ. For we are not born Christians. Innocence, or freedom from actual transgression, is the utmost we can claim, which is a very different thing from moral excellence or righteousness. This must come from the discipline of life, and to accomplish it is precisely the purpose of our being placed in the present state of probation.

Thirdly: The manner and process of this change, of this spiritual development and growth, are very different in different individuals; — as different as men's natural constitutions and the circumstances under which they are placed. To prescribe an invariable rule by which the spiritual experience of all shall be governed, is nothing but religious empiricism, and is the mark of a narrow-minded teacher. It is not necessary that all should walk in the same company and wear the same badge, to be followers of the same Master.

Fourthly: In the formation of our religious character, which is our Regeneration, we are chiefly indebted, as we are in every thing, to the Divine guidance and help. Without God, we are nothing and can do nothing. But we too must work. His working is through our working, nor can we, generally speaking, separate the one from the other. The operation of the Divine Spirit is real and effectual: but as " the wind bloweth where it listeth, and we hear the sound thereof, but cannot tell whence it cometh or whither it goeth, so is every one born of the Spirit."

Finally: The proof of Regeneration is in the life. "Let no man deceive you; he that doeth righteousness is righteous, even as he is righteous." (1 John iii. 7.) It is not in professions, nor in ecstasies, nor in flaming zeal, much less in the self-righteous condemnation of others; but in a life of genuine goodness, purity, and truth. The evidence of the Christian spirit is in the Christian character. By their fruits shall ye know them. " Pure religion and undefiled before God the Father is this, To visit the fatherless and widows in their affliction, and to keep ourselves unspotted from the world."

RETRIBUTION.

THE STING OF DEATH IS SIN; AND THE STRENGTH OF SIN IS THE LAW. BUT THANKS BE TO GOD, WHICH GIVETH US THE VICTORY THROUGH OUR LORD JESUS CHRIST THEREFORE, MY BELOVED BRETHREN, BE YE STEADFAST, UNMOVABLE, ALWAYS ABOUNDING IN THE WORK OF THE LORD, FORASMUCH AS YE KNOW THAT YOUR LABOR IS NOT IN VAIN IN THE LORD.
1 Cor xv. 56-58.

The subject of my present discourse is the doctrine of Future Retribution. If nothing had been said in the Bible directly concerning it, I think that it might be inferred from the manner in which the sacred writers speak of sin as the great evil, and of salvation from it as the great redemption. The whole Gospel dispensation implies that there is a terrible danger to which we are exposed through sin, and a glorious deliverance which is offered through Jesus Christ. 'Who shall deliver me," said the Apostle, " from the body of this death? I thank God, through Jesus Christ our Lord. There is, therefore, now no condemnation to them who are in Christ Jesus. For the law of the spirit of life in him, hath made me free from the law of sin and death." This is the uniform tone in which the Scriptures speak of sin and redemption. I cannot understand it, unless the consequences of sin extend to the future life.

If they were confined to this world, sin would be comparatively a small evil. If they were found only in the occasional loss of friends and of health, or even if they extended so far as to make the whole of the present life miserable, yet if death were sure to bring the end of all, nay, if it were in our power to seek death ourselves, and thereby to open for the weary soul the never-ending bliss of heaven, we might look upon sin itself with feelings comparatively calm and quiet. It would be sad to see the degradation of those who barter their present happiness for debasing pleasures. It would be sad to think of the years which they waste, of the shame which they bring upon themselves and their kindred. But if we could say to them, "The degradation shall soon be changed to infinite glory, the shame shall soon pass into rejoicing, the fire which conscience has kindled shall soon be quenched in the stream which separates time from eternity," the remaining evil might be easily borne. If we could say to him who is now striving to make himself a brute, and who succeeds in making himself a fiend, "Do your very worst; drink of the cup of iniquity to its dregs; bury your soul in earthly lusts, until none but the eye of God can discern that a soul is there; yet, when a few short years are past, thou shalt lie down in the sleep of death, from which thou shalt awake an angel of God pure and spotless," — our feelings with regard to sin and the sinner would be entirely changed. Sin would still be an evil, but how much less than it now appears. It would stand among other evils, like ignorance, or poverty; a serious evil, greater perhaps than the rest, and carefully to be avoided, but at the worst only temporary, and soon to be followed by infinite good. How different are our feelings when we think of it as the beginning here of what must continue hereafter; when we think that a sinful life works in the soul a character which remains after the body dies when we think of that poor, degraded spirit, passing from a life of shame and guilt into a life where it is incapable of receiving any reward except " the things done in the body "; when we think that he who has already forfeited all the best happiness of this life, has nothing to look forward to, except to reap that which he has sown, the fearful looking for of judgment!

I would not underrate the evil of sin in its present development. The wasted features of the drunkard, the cold and malignant look of the gambler, the mean and tricky glance of the thief, the sensual expression of the licentious, the bloodthirsty eye of the murderer, — these are terrible to look upon. We shrink from them with loathing and disgust. The way of the transgressor is hard; his sins punish themselves, and the baseness to which they bring him is fearful. But our horror is increased, while at the same time we are filled with unutterable pity, when we are taught that this is but the beginning of sorrow. O my God, what must be the awaking from such a sleep as this! with every faculty of thought degraded; with every desire made corrupt; with the tastes perverted from good and fixed upon evil; with selfishness as the only rule of action and sin the only object of pursuit; with not even enough of goodness left to make him repent of the wrong done, and throw himself, with cries for pardon, upon the mercies of his God!

Being such a one, when he passes from this life to the future, where shall the sinner appear? What has he to do with the pure and good? What enjoyment can he find in holiness and truth? How can he enter upon the service of God, that heavenly service, which begins in self-renunciation, and is perfected in love? Place him among the just made perfect, who hunger and thirst after righteousness, among the pure in heart, the peacemakers, and what companionship would he find? Alas! it is not the suffering which sin brings with it now, although its present retribution is severe, — it is not this, but the ruin which it works in the soul itself, that makes it so terrible. The present evil soon must cease, but the ruin remains.

It will be seen from my manner of speaking, that the retribution in which I believe is both present and future. It is the execution, now and hereafter, of the laws under which we live: laws which were made in wisdom, and which are executed with apparent sternness, but in real love. Many persons take for granted that by proving a law of retribution in this life, under which we suffer for wrong-doing, they disprove the existence of such a law in the world to come. I think they are in error. The existence of such a law here is a proof that it will continue there. It is the same soul that passes from time to eternity, the same God reigns there and here, the same great purposes are to be accomplished, and we have reason to believe that the same principles of moral government will continue. I would be at pains, therefore, in proving the doctrine of future retribution, to make the fact of present retribution prominent and clear. By doing this, we shall at the same time prove the existence of a general law, under which we now live, and which we have no right to suppose will be abrogated by death; and we shall also see that the operation of this law is here so imperfect, so often interrupted by causes which must evidently cease with the present life, that there is still stronger reason to believe that, in a higher sphere of action, the essential laws of our being will find their more perfect development.

Retribution here is of several kinds. First is that which

we suffer, not as human beings, but in common with all the animal creation. We may call it natural retribution. There are certain laws, the observance of which is essential to continued life and health. Food of a proper kind and in sufficient quantity must be provided; that which is unwholesome must be avoided; the strength must be matured by exercise, and not over-exerted; and other laws of our physical nature must be observed, or evil consequences result. There are similar conditions on which the healthful development of the mind depends. If it is brought too early or too strongly into action, if it is devel oped too rapidly and without regard to the equal claims of the body, not only is the bodily health lost, but the mind also too often becomes unsound, the powers of thought weakened, and the balance of judgment destroyed. Or if the mind is left indolent, if it is suffered to remain torpid or uneducated, the physical nature is brutalized and its real vigor ultimately lost. There are laws, therefore, which belong to the body, and there are laws upon which the healthful connection between the body and the mind depends. Their violation must always bring loss and suffering, to a greater or less degree, for wherever law exists, penalty for its violation must be annexed.

But of these laws we must observe two things, important to our present subject; first, the penalty annexed is just the same, whether their violation is attended with guilt or not. It may be voluntary or involuntary, yet the suffering will be the same. It may come in the performance of unavoidable duty, yet its severity is not relaxed. You may rush into a burning house, to rescue a child from death, yet you will come out with a scarred and tortured body, as much as if you had exposed yourself to the same danger in wantonness, or in the commission of crime. If you are so ignorant of the laws of physical health as to spend all your days in the closet, and rob the nights of sleep, cheating the body of needful exercise and wholesome food, stimulating the brain with hurtful drugs which destroy the nerves, the consequence will be equally certain and severe, whether the folly has been committed in the pursuit of knowledge, of pleasure, or of gain. If you over-exert your strength, though it may be in support of a widowed mother, in the care of the sick, in works of philanthropy, or in the service of religion, yet the consequence will be an invalid frame and premature death, just as certainly as f the same over-exertion had been induced by avarice or ambition. Unnatural and long-continued excitement will produce insanity, whether it is in the church, in the ballroom, or at the gambling-table.

These are facts which, however startling, cannot be denied. The retribution, therefore, of which we now speak, is not moral retribution. It comes not in punishment of guilt nor in reward of virtue. It may indeed be mingled with moral retribution, and may often seem to come as the punishment of guilt. But in itself considered it has no regard to merit or demerit. Ignorance will not exempt us from it; the best intention will not enable us to avoid it.

We observe, secondly, that, so far as human judgment can discern, this retribution is not impartial. Some men are endowed with a physical constitution so strong and elastic, that the utmost irregularities seem to do them no harm; others are so weak, that the slightest departure from prudence brings suffering or death. The same degree ot indulgence which, in one family, will make children victims of disease, will, in another, be consistent with their vigorous and healthy growth. And so in all the departments of life, the bad results, under the law we now con sider, not only come without regard to the intention of the offender, but, so far as we can see, bear no equal proportion to the offence itself. I have no doubt, that, if we were able to take a view of the whole, it would seem otherwise; for the circumstances which produce these apparent inequalities are, perhaps, themselves the result of previous action of the same laws. The frail constitution may be the result of some violation of physical law by our parents, or by our ancestry a hundred years ago. The causes, which in one family produce disease and in another do no harm, seem to us the same, but, through some influence unknown to us, may be entirely different. Still, so far as moral government is concerned, the effect upon individuals is the same. The retribution is not impartial. It comes upon us like blows struck in the dark. The comparatively guilty escape, the comparatively innocent suffer. It may serve under our present subject as an illustration of a general law, but it is not the kind of retribution needed for moral discipline.

There is a SECOND kind of retribution which we may call social. It consists in the loss of reputation, of friends, of social position, and of every thing outward which makes life pleasant or desirable. The drunkard becomes an object of disgust, and the finger of scorn is pointed at him. The licentious man is marked as one to be avoided. The thief is branded with a harsh epithet and immured in the walls of a prison. Public opinion, the usages of society, the criminal code, the laws of friendship and kindred, all minister to this social retribution of wrong-doing. If the usages of society were always correct, if human laws were perfect and perfectly administered, if public opinion were sound and in accordance with Christian principles, this retribution would go far to answer all the purposes of moral discipline. But unfortunately, nothing can be more unequal, more arbitrary, or unjust. Taking the world as it is, looking at the facts as they really are, the social retribution visited upon crime, so far from answering the purpose of moral discipline, is one of the greatest obstacles in its way. Society does not punish sin according to its real enormity, but to the circumstances under which it is committed. This is done, not by any rule of justice, but in the most partial and tyrannical manner. Those who have the least excuse for crime are most likely to escape punishment, while those whose temptations were so great that resistance was almost impossible, are punished to the utmost extent of the law, and exposed to the worst censure of public opinion. Children, who grow up in some den of iniquity, whose parents praise them when they steal and punish them when they are honest, who are educated by all the influences around them to become the pests of society, when they are a little older commit some felony or some act of violence, and for a theft of a few dollars are sent to the penitentiary for two or three years, from which they come out, with almost no possibility before them but a life of wickedness and shame. How different is the sentence which society passes upon the man who, in his childhood, had every advantage of Christian education and good example, and who has grown up among influences which make virtue easy and remove the worst temptations of vice! Such a man, when guilty, we do not now say of theft, but of peculation to a hundred times the amount, under circumstances, perhaps, where there is the most inexcusable breach of trust, and the most heartless wrong committed against his best friends, will escape comparatively unpunished. There may be a temporary loss of credit, but if he has been successful in his villany, it all comes right with him very soon; he is again numbered among the respectable men of the community, and his children grow up in the best society.

We might give a thousand illustrations of the same sort. The gambler, who stakes a few dollars on a throw and whose sphere of action is low and vulgar, is called by his right name and regarded with the contempt which he deserves. But he who is able to stake thousands, and whose gambling-table stands in the carpeted room of a gentleman's residence, may be guilty of the same crime without losing caste and almost without censure. Intemperance in the rich is a very different thing from intemperance in the poor. And so it happens that the advantages of social position, which make the sin itself greater, shield the sinner from the punishment he deserves. Society is full of such injustice. The tribunal of public opinion is one where a bribe is never refused.

It is evident, therefore, that neither natural nor social retribution is sufficient for the purposes of moral discipline. We need a retribution which is certain, impartial, and in exact proportion to the guilt committed. And this leads us to consider a THIRD kind of retribution, which, beginning in this world, will be perfected in the world to come, — the retribution of conscience. It certainly begins here. We never commit sin intentionally without feeling rebuked for it and sometimes the punishment which a sensitive conscience inflicts is so severe, that it seems beyond the offence committed.

There are some who believe that this retribution of conscience is perfect and complete in the present life; that every sin is certainly punished, and in exact proportion to the degree of guilt; but I cannot agree with them. Neither my experience nor my observation confirms it. I am willing to admit that the tendency of this retribution is to become more and more just. If all adventitious circumstances were removed, if conscience had a fair and open field of action, its decisions would be just and in all cases governed by the offence. But this I believe rarely takes place in this world. Practically speaking, its decisions are continually warped and its sentence is continually avoided: so that, although it gives plain indication of what it may become in the future life, it is at present an uncertain and insufficient tribunal. For in the first place, it is more or less quick and severe in its action, according to the physical constitution. The man of sensitive nerves and delicate frame has a conscience so tender, that every slight departure from duty gives him pain, and often it becomes so morbid, that he is kept in constant misery, where no wrong has been intended. Others, naturally of a coarser temperament, have no desire to be better than their neighbors, and live in the daily commission of faults, without the least self-reproach.

Again, the circumstance of failure or success has a strange effect upon the decisions of conscience, although it can have none upon the act itself. A course of iniquity which happens to end in good results, fails to excite those severe compunctions which would have arisen from the same crime if unsuccessful. A fraud which makes me rich, does not trouble me so much as the same fraud, when it makes me poor. Only in the latter case does conscience see and declare the truth.

In the same manner, the concealment of sin often keeps the conscience comparatively quiet, through long years, even to the end of life; when, if it had been revealed to the world, and the scorn of good men and the estrangement of friends had been thereby visited upon us, conscience would at the same time have awaked, like a wild beast from his lair, to rend our hearts in pieces. It seems as if the veil of secrecy hides the fault, not only from the eyes of others, but from our own. Discovery is needed to show us what we are. Yet it is evident that continued concealment sometimes increases the sin by the added guilt of hypocrisy.

Add to these things the complication which comes from the unequal working of the natural and social retribution to which we have already referred. The decisions of conscience are continually overborne by influences beyond its control. We easily reconcile ourselves to sins which are countenanced in society. The whisperings of conscience are hushed, and we forget to condemn ourselves for doing what others do. The individual conscience rarely speaks, but instead of it a conventional or average conscience, which is far less sensitive and correct. The external rewards of life come with so unequal regard to our real deserving, we are so often sufferers in ourselves and in our families, for actions well intended and in themselves right, that it requires a degree of faithfulness which few men exercise, to keep the conscience itself from being hardened or perverted.

It is easy to say that the consciousness of right rewards us sufficiently, let the loss and suffering be what they may; but to make it so requires a degree of moral elevation seldom attained. If we analyze our feelings in times of such experience, we shall find that it is not the present award of conscience which upholds us, so much as the belief that its sentence will be confirmed hereafter. We rest patiently under the loss, we cheerfully endure the pain, because we are assured that the victory now accomplished is an eternal victory, and that the light affliction, which is but for the moment, is working for us a far more exceeding, even an eternal weight of glory. This demands our careful consid eration. The healthy action of conscience in the present life depends upon our belief that the consequences of sin extend to the future. It is this belief which shows the enormity of sin and the real injury it does to the soul. I do not advocate a slavish fear of punishment, but I believe that the retribution which conscience now imposes is derived, in a great part, from the knowledge that it will go on to its perfect fulfilment beyond the grave. It is, therefore, although a present retribution, chiefly the anticipation of the future.

There is another kind of moral retribution, which comes from the application of the general law to our moral nature. It consists in the formation of character. By our manner of life, the soul is moulded into certain shapes of beauty or deformity; its capacities enlarged or contracted; its perceptions quickened or made dull; its tastes purified or debased; its inward life made heavenly or vile. We therefore suffer retribution by what we are. The present character for good or evil is retributive of the past. Each day lays up for the morrow a retribution which is absolutely sure to come. It is also progressive and cumulative, for the present character is the result of all that has gone before. In this manner, as we enter upon each successive stage of life, from childhood to youth, from youth to manhood, from manhood to mature and advancing age, we carry with us the results of the past, — an actual retribution, in the moral habits, in the greater or less development of the mind, in the actual, although acquired, nature of the soul.

This also, like the direct retribution of conscience, would be in exact accordance with justice, were there no disturbing influences. But in fact, we are not the absolute framers of our own character. The moral position in which we stand is not altogether the result of our own merit or demerit. We are moulded as much by the influences of education and early example, of country and climate and other external forces, as by our own exertions. Our present character, therefore, being the consequence of all that has gone before, may be considered under the natural law as an exact retribution of the past. But under the moral law, which has regard only to moral desert, it is very far from being a just or impartial award.

I am well aware that considerations such as I have now brought forward lead us into a labyrinth of thought, from which we cannot alone find a return. If we imagine ourselves to be placed upon the seat of judgment, to pass sentence upon each individual according to his real desert, we must acknowledge that to our finite faculties the task would be impossible. It is a work which belongs only to an infinite mind. God alone can discern the real truth in every heart. He alone can untangle the perplexed thread of life, so that each one shall feel that he is fairly dealt with, according to the deeds done in the body, whether they be good or evil. For this reason, there are no circumstances under which we should dare to anticipate the judgment of God. As the poor widow, who cast in one mite, was said to have given more than all the rest, because it was more in proportion to her ability, so may it often be in God's judgment, when our full account is rendered. The seeming saint and the despised sinner may then change places; "the last shall be the first, and the first last." It is for God alone to administer and execute the laws which God alone has made. But although it would be arrogant in us to assume his place as many do, in pronouncing sentence upon the offender, we may yet believe that in the infinite wisdom of God a just sentence shall be pronounced. We may perceive that there are principles of justice, applicable to every case, although we are not competent to app.y them. We may rest satisfied in believing that God is greater than the heart and knoweth all things. He who is the Judge of all the earth will do only that which is right.

From the course of thought which we have now followed, as the result of experience and observation, we arrive at these conclusions. First, that the great law of our lives is the law of retribution. The present is answering for the past, the future must answer for the present. God's laws cannot be violated with impunity. That which we sow, we also reap. This, in its various developments, is the primal, essential law of our being. Secondly, considered as a moral retribution, the action of this great law is, in this world, imperfect and unequal. The disturbing influences are so many, that, although we may discern a tendency towards justice, impartial justice is not here attained. The punishment of sin is not according to the degree of sin, but is made greater or less by a thousand circumstances, which do not affect the degree of guilt. Thirdly, both of these conclusions lead us to a third, namely, that the same general law of retribution, which seems to be the condition of life itself, shall continue in the soul as long as the soul lives. There is nothing to indicate that it belongs to this world only. Let the fact of a future life be admitted, and it seems to follow, as a matter of necessity, that this law shall continue. If so, it will become, as a moral retribution, just and equal. The disturbing influences will cease. They belong only to a state of probation, the infancy of the soul's life, and will have no place there. Here we see through a glass darkly, there face to face. The principles of God's moral government, which are here but imperfectly developed, will there obtain a full and perfect administration. Such is the logical conclusion with regard to the future from the premises given here.

It seems to me, therefore, that when we come to the Gospel, as the revelation of God, we do not so much need that the law of retribution should be announced or confirmed, as that it should be restrained. It is a law so absolute, so radical, so unsparing, so fearful, that we can find no escape from it. Under the light of reason alone, scarcely any hope is given; we find no shelter from the impending wrath. He who believes in a future life, and who sees the stern, relentless law under which the soul now lives, — a law whose present execution is stayed, but still threatens to come when the soul is exposed defenceless to its power, — does not need to be told of the terrors of the Lord, so much as of his forbearance and loving-kindness and tender mercy. We need to be taught, not so much that destruction is impending, as that a way of escape is provided. I confess that, as a believer in eternity, if reason were my only guide, I should shudder whenever I think of death. Then indeed it would be a "fearful thing to fall into the hands of the living God." A dim and uncertain hope of his mercy might come, to save us from absolute despair, but the sins that rise up in judgment against us are so many, that we need an assurance of pardon, almost before we dare to hope. It is this assurance that the Gospel gives. It teaches that through the redemption in Jesus Christ, a limit to that fearful law of retribution is found. There is forgiveness with God. He will not exact the payment of the uttermost farthing, but will freely forgive us " all that debt." To make this known was the great object of Christ's coming. As it is written, " the law came by Moses, but grace and truth by our Lord Jesus Christ." It is the Gospel of redemption, not of condemnation. It came to inspire hope, not to increase despair. It changes the law of retribution, under which we reap only that which we sow, to a law of reconciliation, under which all estrangement from God, the worst penalty of sin, is removed, and the returning prodigal is restored to the arms of a father's love.

But to whom is this promise given? To whom is this pardon offered? Even in his mercy God is just, and while a way of escape for the sinner is provided, his condemnation upon sin remains.

There is no passage in the Bible, so far as I know, which offers pardon, except on condition of repentance and a renewed life. If there is any exception to this, it is where faith in Christ is declared the sole condition of eternal life. But those who understand the meaning of faith, in the New Testament, know that it is a state of mind and character, which includes repentance and self-consecration to God. The third chapter of the Gospel of John insists equally upon the necessity of the new birth and upon the supreme importance of faith in Christ. They both imply the same spiritual experience which is the condition on which forgiveness is promised.

I state this, therefore, as the First Scriptural argument for the continuance of the law of retribution in the future life; namely, that although the great object of the Gospel is to reveal the mercy of God and his willingness to forgive, ye we are encouraged to hope for pardon only upon the condition which I have named. The inference is most plain, tha to those who continue in sin forgiveness is not offered They abide under the law of condemnation from which they refuse to escape.

Another Scriptural argument to the same effect is found in the manner in which the doctrine of future retribution is often taken for granted, as the basis on which instruction is given. When the Saviour says, " He that loses his life for my sake shall find it," we can give no full meaning to his words, except on the supposition that, although we lose every thing in this life, we gain more in the future. If that future were the same to us, whether we are faithful or unfaithful here, his words would scarcely have been true. When the Scripture says, " Be thou faithful unto death, and I will give thee a crown of life," we are plainly taught that to those who are unfaithful that crown is not offered. In the chapter from which my text is taken, the object of the Apostle is simply to prove the doctrine of a future life. He says nothing directly of retribution, but declares that all of us shall be raised again by the power of God in such a body as may please him. Yet he concludes his discourse with the words, " Therefore be ye steadfast, unmovable, always abounding in the work of the Lord, forasmuch as ye know that your labor is not in vain in the Lord." Therefore? why? Why is the fact of a future life an argument for our being steadfast and unmovable? Because the future must answer for the present. Because the pure in heart alone can see God. Because we have no right to hope for acceptance, unless we can comply with the conditions on which it is offered. Believing this, we know that our labor is not in vain in the Lord. But if good and bad shall appear before him, in equal glory and in equal favor, the Apostle's words seem to me without force, and the motive which he urges for our faithfulness is taken away.

We might give many other instances like this. Even the prodigal son is required to return, with the words of confession on his lips and with a heart full of penitence, before his father comes out to meet him. A broad distinction is made between the good and bad, the penitent and impenitent, whenever a future life is mentioned, and it is taken for granted that it will continue there. I attach more importance to this form of argument than I do to the literal interpretation of words, and think that it is much less likely to mislead us. The plainest language may be explained away, and we may be deceived as to its meaning. But this argument does not depend on verbal criticism. When the doctrine of a future life is used as a motive for faithfulness and obedience, it is an evident declaration, that that un known world is not the same to the good and bad, but that the future must answer for the present.

Thirdly, there are, however, many direct assertions of the same truth. The ingenuity of criticism may throw a doubt over some of them, but they are so many, and their obvious interpretation seems to me so evidently their true meaning, that, although I would not impute intentional unfairness to those who explain them away, I cannot help feeling surprised at the boldness of their undertaking. "Except your righteousness shall exceed that of the Scribes and Pharisees ye shall in no case enter into the kingdom of heaven." "If ye forgive not men their trespasses, neither will your Father in heaven forgive your trespasses." "Not every one that saith unto me, Lord, Lord, shall enter into the kingdom of heaven, but he who doeth the will of my Father which is in heaven." "Fear not them which kill the body, but are not able to kill the soul, but rather fear him who is able to destroy both soul and body in hell." "For we must all appear," said the Apostle Paul, "before the judgment-seat of Christ, that every one may receive the things done in his body, according to that he hath done, whether it be good or bad." "Know this, that no unclean person hath any inheritance in the kingdom of Christ and of God." Again, after enumerating the works of the flesh, he says "Of the which I tell you before, as I have also told you in times past, that they who do such things shall not inherit the kingdom of God." For "God will render to every man according to his deeds; to them who, by patient continuance in well-doing, seek for glory and honor and immortality, eternal life. But unto them that are contentious and do not obey the truth, but obey unrighteousness, indignation and wrath, tribulation and anguish, upon every soul of man that doeth evil, of the Jew first and also of the Gentile ; but glory, honor, and peace to every man that worketh good, to the Jew first, and also to the Gentile; for there is no respect of persons with God " " For the wages of sin is death, but the gift of God is eternal life through Jesus Christ our Lord."

I do not see how this language can be fairly explained, except as teaching the doctrine of future retribution for sin. So far as I can understand their words, this is what the Saviour and his Apostles meant to teach, and therefore I believe it.

It is important for me here to refer more particularly to the Scripture use of the word Hell, because it not only affords an argument for the doctrine to be proved, but also removes some of the most popular objections brought against it. In the Old Testament the word, properly speaking, never occurs, for although we find it in our translation, the original word in Hebrew is SHEOL, which corresponds with the Greek word HADES, and means the place of departed spirits, or the grave. See Gen. xxxvii. 35; xlii. 38; where it is so translated, and we have the authority of the Septuagint for the same translation in all cases.

In the common version of the New Testament, it occurs twenty times. In ten of which the Greek word is Hades, and should have been accordingly translated. See Luke xvi. 23; Acts ii. 31; and elsewhere. In the other ten passages where the word occurs, the original is not HADES, but GEHENNA, by looking at which we shall understand most of the language applied by Scripture to the punishment of the wicked. It is a Hebrew word properly signifying the valley of Hinnom, a beautiful val ey near Jerusalem, by the brook Kidron, where Solomon at the time of his apostasy from God set up a brazen image of Moloch, before which the idolatrous Jews offered, not only the usual sacrifices, but even their own children. 1 Kings xi. 7; 2 Chron. xxviii. 3. This valley was called by the prophet Jeremiah, Tophet, Jer. vii. 31, 32, from a word signifying Tympanum, because in those sacrifices the priests beat violently the Tympana, lest the shrieks of the burning children should be heard by the worshippers. When these horrible rites were abolished by Josias, 2 Kings xxiii. 10, and the Jews were reclaimed to the worship of God, they detested this valley, the scene of their guilt, so much, that they made it the receptacle, not only of all the filth of the city, but of dead animals and of the bodies of executed criminals; and to prevent the pollution of the air from this mass of decayed matter, fires were kept incessantly burning, night and day, from the beginning to the end of the year. Hence, the valley of Hinnom or Gehenna soon passed into a proverb or common expression for any severe punishment, and especially for any disgraceful kind of death, and ultimately was applied to the miserable condition of those who, in the future life, suffer the agonies of guilt; so that, in the time of Christ, one of the common meanings of Gehenna was what we understand by the word Hell.*

This, however, was not its only use, and therefore, in

---

* "The word Gehenna is used in this way (viz. for the place of punishment beyond the grave) very frequently in Oriental writers, as far as India. Compare Wetstein's New Testament, at Matt. v 22' --Jahn's Archæology, § 411.

reading the New Testament, we must be guided by the context to determine the meaning in each case. But in several of the passages it undoubtedly refers to the doom of the wicked; as in the text already quoted, "Fear him who is able to destroy both soul and body in hell," Matt. x. 28, any other construction of which seems to me very forced and unnatural.

This word Gehenna, derived as I have shown it to be, but transferred from its original meaning and applied to express figuratively the condition of the wicked, contains in itself the germ and explanation of all the various terms which the Scriptures use to describe future punishment. To call the abode of the condemned Gehenna, to a Jewish ear included the fire which is never quenched, and the undying worm, and the lake of fire burning with brimstone. These particulars were only the completion of the first idea. To us they seem to add a great deal to the simple term Gehenna, but to a Jew that word embraced within itself all that is horrible and loathsome, all that is disgraceful and revolting, all that is agonizing, in ignominious punishment and death. To the application of this term to the place of punishment, we may therefore with certainty attribute those figurative expressions, in which it is spoken of as a place of darkness and fierce burning and torture. All these expressions are figures derived from that awful valley, whose name was borrowed to describe the state of being we call Hell.

I call them figures, in which probably few persons will disagree with me. The believers in a hell of literal fire and brimstone are fast passing away. It is an idea too gross, too shocking, to be long retained by a civilized and educated people. There is something so like savage cruelty in the thought of casting a living being into eternal flames, to live for ever the prey of devouring but never destroying fire, that we instinctively shrink from it, as unworthy of a good and wise God. It is astonishing to me that for so long a time men clung to this literal language and insisted upon the existence of the lake of fire and brimstone, in which the body is tormented; and that even now, the favorite mode of bringing men to God is by holding up a picture of exquisitely contrived torture, to scare their imaginations and frighten them out of sin. It is called preaching the terrors of the Lord. But I do not believe that God means to arm those who preach his word with a whip of scorpions by which to drive men to heaven. He has given us no authority to represent him as a cruel, unfeeling, relentless being, who looks with complacency upon the miserable victims of ceaseless burning. The effect of such representations is to create distrust of all retribution. It becomes associated with so much that is horrible and disgusting, it is made to appear so unlike that treatment which we have a right to expect from a just and merciful God, that we turn our minds away from it and refuse belief in the truth itself.

But let me not be misunderstood. I would not lessen the fear which sin brings to the guilty man. It cannot be too great, so long as it is calm and rational, arising from our knowledge of the ruin which sin brings upon the soul now, and the dread of what it may do hereafter. The terms used by the Scripture, though strongly figurative, are not unmeaning words. We may divest ourselves of the horror which their literal interpretation would convey, but we cannot set them aside. The Saviour, in adopting as the expression for the punishment of the wicked a word so full of terror as the valley of Hinnom, took the surest way of declaring that the sorrow of the sinful soul hereafter is beyond the power of tame words to describe.

Figurative language is used to convey greater strength and intensity of meaning. Are we yet so ignorant as not to know, so brutish as not to understand, that there is no torture of these frail sinews, no agony which can be brought on this crumbling body, so dreadful as the rising of an abused conscience to assert its stern dominion over the guilty soul. There are hundreds of instances in this world, where the perpetrators of heinous crimes have fled to the punishment of the dungeon and the gallows, as if to a mother's arms, because they could no longer bear the secret lashing of their conscience. And, on the other hand, there are those who so value the peace of mind which a conscience void of offence brings, that they would not barter it for all earthly good, nor lose it to avoid the worst and longest torture which the body is able to endure. There is a story of an English martyr, who, when bound to the stake, held his right hand in the fire until it was burned off, declaring that the hand which had signed his recantation should suffer first. The pain of his body was nothing compared with the anguish of his mind.

Such things go far to explain the figurative language of the Scripture. The stings of guilt are not easily to be borne. Who has not felt enough in his own heart to know this? If we wished to picture to ourselves the real climax of suffering, it would be to place the soul, not in outward fire, but in the midst of beauty and external delight, with this curse upon it, that neither day nor night should the serpent teeth of remorse cease to gnaw and devour. That curse would convert all things into instruments o. torture, and outward flames would not be wanting to increase the woe.

The principal argument against the doctrine of future punishment is founded upon mistaken ideas of God's benevolence. If he is a good being, — it is urged, — if he is our Heavenly Father, how is it possible that such dreadful suffering can be in store for any of his creatures?

There are some theories of future punishment, as we have already seen, against which this objection may be fairly brought. When God is represented as a vindictive being, who for his own glory appoints a large part of his human family to the endurance of eternal and hopeless suffering, in punishment for sins committed in these few years of mortal life, we cannot reconcile it with his goodness and his love. I cannot believe that any part of his creatures are subject to a destiny so terrible as this. But on the other hand, we should remember that our knowledge of the Divine attributes, and of the real claims of justice and mercy, is very limited. God seeth not as man seeth, for he sees the whole and man only a part. It may hereafter appear that many things which seem to us inconsistent with God's love, are in fact its most perfect exercise.

The goodness of God, according to the teaching of Scripture and of enlightened reason, is not the goodness of indulgence and weakness. It is that of a wise Father, who seeks the real good of his children. Which one of us, who is a parent, would not consent to the infliction of the severest pain for months and years upon his child, if it were needful to save him from drunkenness or dishonesty? What degree of suffering would not be considered a blessing, in the accomplishment of a work like this? And so, in the dealings of our Heavenly Father towards us. Even in this world, we see many instances in which the Divine love does not shrink from the infliction of long-continued and terrible suffering, as the punishment of sin, or for the purification of the soul. Sometimes we can see the reason of such inflictions; sometimes they are so veiled in mystery that we can explain them only by saying, that in the future world what is now dark will be made clear. In such cases, however, we do not think of disputing the Divine benevolence, but say that there are undoubtedly sufficient reasons for whatever suffering may come, and that it is intended for the good of those who bear it. Why should not the same faith in Divine goodness extend to the future world? The real life of the soul can be found only in purity and truth, and whatever degree of suffering may be needful, either in this world or in the world to come, for our education therein, should be considered as a proof of the highest love. If the way to goodness lies through suffering and pain, it is the part of kindness to lead us there. If it is true that the soul shall live for ever, and is capable of the highest exaltation through holiness and the lowest degradation through sin; if its dignity and true happiness can be found only in voluntary obedience to the will of God, — then we can understand how the paternal love of God may subject us to a law of retribution, which seems stern and terrible, but which is the chastening of a Father's hand.

But it will be asked, How is such a theory as this consistent with the doctrine of *eternal* punishment? If the suffering is inflicted for the sake of him who suffers, must it not have an end? Must not a day come for the final restoration of all? And if so, what does the Scripture mean when it speaks of "endless punishment," and "the fire that never dies"? I would answer these questions with diffidence, and do not seek to be wise above what is written.

There are certainly some passages of Scripture which seem to imply that the time will come, when all resistance to the power of God shall cease, and all souls be brought under subjection to the word of Christ; a subjection which cannot be perfect, except through willing obedience. Nor is the use of the word "eternal," with reference to future suffering, an absolute contradiction of this view; for it can be plainly shown that that word, and others like it, are frequently used in the Bible with reference to limited duration It is almost certain, indeed, that there was no word in the Hebrew or Greek language, which conveyed to those who used it the idea which we now conceive of absolute eternity.

But on the other hand, it is also true that the strongest words which those languages afford were applied to future punishment, and are the same which are applied to the promises of future happiness.

Again, although there are some hints given of a final restoration of all things, and although our belief in the paternal goodness of God seems to lead to the same result, yet there are obvious difficulties in the way. By the nature of the soul, its return to goodness must be voluntary. It cannot be compelled, even for its own benefit, without a destruction of its best capacities. The same voluntary resistance to God which is begun here, may therefore continue through unknown ages, and we have no right to expect that God will ever impose upon us a necessity of being good. It is therefore a fearful risk which we run, in suffering ourselves to become more and more hardened in sin. We do not know how far the capacity of goodness may die. We do not know but that we may separate ourselves so far from God, as to make our return impossible. Such thoughts are well calculated to awaken fear and trembling. The immortal soul is not to be trifled with, and those who bury it under sin are incurring a risk, greater perhaps than we can understand.

Yet my own disposition inclines to hope. I cannot help

believing that God in his infinite wisdom and goodness will find a way of return for all, without violation of the laws by which the soul lives. At all events, we may be sure that the punishment which he inflicts will never be vindictive. He will never forget a Father's love in the severity of his judgment. No one of his creatures will ever be beyond the reach of his infinite pity.

In entertaining this hope, however, we do not assert that the consequences of long-continued sin, to those who slight the offers of mercy made to us here, will ever completely cease. A wasted life may leave, and it is reasonable to suppose will leave, an ineradicable stain upon the soul. Our capacity of happiness may be thereby for ever lessened. Even if restored to the favor of God, and to a measure of happiness which fills our heart with gratitude to him, we may for ever feel that an irreparable loss has been sustained. For there is no reason to suppose that all who are happy in the world to come enjoy an equal degree of bliss. We may therefore see that there is a sense in which the consequences of a sinful life may be an eternal retribution, without violence to God's goodness and mercy.

But I never engage in speculations such as these, without feeling how completely they are beyond my reach. They give me little satisfaction or concern, and I have now entered upon them more for the sake of frankness than any thing else. The Scriptures teach that forgiveness of sin is freely offered to all who comply with the conditions of the Gospel of Christ; that to those who will not comply with such conditions, but continue in a sinful and impenitent life, a just and severe retribution is appointed in the future world; that the Saviour to whom all judgment is committed, is the same who died for us; and that the God from whom all judgment comes, is our Heavenly Father Thus far the instruction is plain, and to my mind unquestionable I do not seek to go beyond it.

There are many questions which we naturally ask, but to which the Scripture gives no complete answer. When the disciples inquired, "Are there few that be saved?" Jesus said, "STRIVE YE to enter in at the strait gate"; and this is to all of us the only practical and needful reply. The secrets of the unknown world are but imperfectly revealed, but we know enough for our present guidance, enough to inspire hope and to awaken fear. The hope rests upon God's mercy, the fear looks to his justice; but they unite to lead us in the paths of righteousness, for the mercy and the justice of God are alike inseparable from a Father's love. "Therefore, my beloved brethren, be ye steadfast, unmovable, always abounding in the work of the Lord, forasmuch as ye know that your labor is not in vain in the Lord."

www.ingramcontent.com/pod-product-compliance
Lightning Source LLC
Chambersburg PA
CBHW022117160426
43197CB00009B/1064